A Stroll In The Country

Written and illustrated
by
Henry Brewis

Published by Powdene Publicity

First published in 1999 by
Powdene Publicity Ltd, Unit 17, St Peter's Wharf,
Newcastle upon Tyne NE6 1TZ. Telephone: (0191) 265 0040

Cover design: Metromedia

Printed by: CDP, Tyne & Wear

British Library Cataloguing in Publication Data

A catalogue record of this book is available from the British Library

ISBN 0 9520226 7 2

By The Same Author

A Load of Rural Rubbish
Any Fool Can Be a Farmer
The Road to Clartiehole
Farmfoolery
Funnywayt'mekalivin'
Don't Laugh till He's out of Sight
The Magic Peasant
Clarts and Calamities (Diary of a Peasant Farmer)
Chewing the Cud
Country Dance
Goodbye Clartiehole
Night Shift
Harvey and the Handy Lads (for children)
Published by Farming Press
Wharfedale Road, Ipswich 1PI 4LG

Also cassettes: Rural Stew and Country Casserole (Bridge Studios, Kirklands,
Scremerston, Berwick-upon-Tweed)
Shepherd's Pie & Second Helpings (Farming Press)

Foreword

LET'S be clear at the start. This is not a seriously important book – and nobody in their right mind would pretend it is . . . except perhaps the author – but you know what authors are like . . .

Obviously it's no epic blockbuster. No steaming pot-boiler stuff here, with pages full of breathless heroines, heaving bosoms, and handsome, heartless heroes, all doing naughty things in exotic locations. Sorry.

It's hardly a learned academic tome either. Not the carefully researched study of some fascinating figure who maybe invented the wheely-bin, conquered India, or rose from deprived single-parent poverty to be chairman of the Parish Council.

And it's definitely not a gripping saga of espionage, intrigue and international chicanery, littered with sinister characters creeping about on the dark side of the world in search of a secret formula to save the planet, or render politicians speechless. What would I know of such things?

So what is it about then? Well, it was all Stewart Bonney's idea really. He's the fellow who edits a rather classy magazine called 'The Northumbrian', a publication enjoyed by a whole host of enlightened folk far and wide, all of whom would claim a deep affection for the countryside – and in particular this noble bit of border Britain. Who've sniffed the rare air and been gently intoxicated by the beauty, the history . . . and maybe even the natives.

'A Stroll In The Country' is simply a collection, a miscellany of pieces written for 'The Northumbrian' over the past few years. A sort of pot-pourri of whatever tickled the writer's imagination at the time. The periodic rural ramblings, if you like, of an umpteenth generation peasant quietly chewing the cud somewhere up the Wansbeck Valley. Memories and whimsy.

It's about farming life (the changes), village life, country life – awkward animals and canny characters who live 'oot bye'. I suppose it has a North-country flavour, right enough – but that needn't worry anyone from the city or the south. You'll surely find something y' fancy. The odd tale to amuse. Barely a gourmet meal perhaps – more a tasty wee snack, easily digested.

Anyway, just dip in when you've got nowt better to do. It'll certainly dee y' nae harm . . .

Henry Brewis

Glossary

bagie	a turnip (sometimes also referred to as snadger or neep).
bait	food, grub...often taken to eat at work.
barred	closed, shut, forbidden.
Blackie	Scottish Blackface...A breed of hill sheep.
blather	to talk incessantly...generally about nowt.
brayed	beaten.
bullet	sweet, confection.
bumler	a bee.
callant	a lad, a youth.
canny	several meanings depending on the context, e.g. quite good, agreeable, shrewd.
Cheviot	a mountain and a breed of sheep, both with similar intellect – though the sheep can move considerably quicker.
clarts	North-country mud.
cleaky mat	cheap, hard wearing, kitchen fireside mat – made from odd bits of old discarded clothing etc, – woven (cleaked) into hessian sacking.
divvent	do not, don't.
donnert	brainless, stupid.
dowta	daughter.
droothy	very dry . . . as in a drought.
durg	dog.
femmer	fragile, frail.
fither	father.
git away bye:	a command to a collie dog (or durg) designed to encourage him (or her) to set off around the flock. The dog may not always return.
gimmer	a young female sheep.
gob	mouth.
grite	great.
haddaway	go away, be off.
Half-Bred	another breed of sheep. A large lowland breed costing a fortune to feed.
hame sticks	part of heavy horse harness, attached to collar and connected to cart or other implement to pull.

hemmel	cattle yard, once used to house cattle in winter. Often converted now to accommodate lawyers and accountants all the year round.
hinney	honey, a term of affection.
hint-end	hind-end or back-side (opposite to fore-end).
howk	dig or poke.
hoy	throw, hurl.
keek	look or peer.
kinlin	small pieces of wood used to light a fire.
muckle	enormous.
Mule	or Greyface sheep . . . particularly dour.
netty	a small building (often found at the bottom of the garden) for private meditation. Also known as the privy.
nowt	nothing.
ower	over.
Percy special:	a potentially lethal concoction of whisky and cherry brandy, much favoured by hunting folk. When consumed in sufficient quantity, it can inspire both horse and rider with a reckless abandon in their pursuit of the fearsome fox – or indeed anything else.
Robson and Cowan:	a remarkable rural emporium tucked away in darkest Northumbria – providing everything the countryman and his missus might require – from welly socks to washing machines, lawnmowers to lamb nuts, chain saws to computers . . .
scraffle	scramble, stumble.
stand on	auctioneer's language . . . meaning 'begin the bidding for this lot – where the preceding lot ended'.
stone	an agricultural word for a testicle.
strite	straight.
taak	talk.
tup	a ram (uncastrated male sheep) . . . who enjoys one orgy per annum.
waal	wall.
watta	water.
wuffler	a remarkable machine which prepares hay for the baling process . . . and encourages rain.
yark	thrash, hit, strike.
yem	home (haddaway yem – go home).
yow	ewe, i.e. a female sheep.

Odd Laddie

LONG ago, when I was no more than a spotty embryo peasant, with a fluffy top lip and teenage delusions of adequacy, I came home from school to work for my father on a farm near Shilbottle. He reckoned it was high time I did something useful. He'd just had the worst winter and the best summer anyone could remember, and a man called Clement Attlee was Prime Minister.

Those were the days before farming became agriculture. It was still a way of life, not yet a plaything for politicians and green environmentalists. The change had begun of course, Hitler's war (like the Kaiser's war and the Napoleonic nonsense) had dragged farming out of the doldrums again. Necessity is the mother of invention especially when the nation is hungry, and sure enough science and subsidy were "persuading" the industry into a new era.

But the real revolution hadn't really happened yet, the EEC jigsaw was still scattered about on the floor, hectares were still acres, kilos were still hundredweights and shepherds had bandy legs and a "useful" collie dog called Sweep. In those days tractors were made of iron with seats that paralysed your bum. Only very few little red combines crawled through the cornfields coughing out railways sacks filled with sixteen stones of wheat.

Stooks, stacks and pikes were still part of the rural vocabulary. There were threshin' days with 20 folk for dinner, and pigkillin' days, followed by a diet of thick fat salty bacon for the rest of your life – and four or five farm hands, where today there may be none.

At Shilbottle father employed a busy little shepherd called Willie who stood no higher than a Suffolk tup, but he could hurl awkward sheep and colourful obscenities further than most men twice his size. The early tranquillity of many a dewy morning was oft times shattered by Willie's instructions to his bewildered dogs, as they tore about in rings trying desperately to please their master. You could hear him from miles away – nervous rabbits went back below ground, sensitive young country maidens on their reluctant way to school blushed and giggled, blackbirds and spuggies broke off the dawn chorus until Willie went home for breakfast, and normal service could be resumed.

Charlie the tractorman was built like a hoose-end, with a similar IQ. I've never come across anyone with such blatant strength. He could carry two bags of corn up the granary steps and whistle at the same time. He also taught me how to clip sheep. It was a very simple method based on the

5

premise that the shearer must impose his will on the twitching victim from the outset and finish the operation as quickly as possible. He would therefore roar into the catching pen, grab the first unfortunate sheep to hand, and promptly give it "a damned good hidin'".

This anaesthetic approach ensured the patient sat very still in a sort of coma, while Charlie whipped the fleece off in three minutes flat. Father said he had a lot of ewes with brain damage as a result of Charlie's violent technique, but most people with any knowledge of sheep will know that this is a biological contradiction. It's a bit like discussing athlete's foot in a worm.

Joe was a canny bloke, very good with horses. We still had three Clydesdales on the farm. Rosie, Prince and Duke were used to pull cartloads of muck and turnips, work in the hayfield and lead corn. They were especially useful in winter when a tractor tended to churn up the wet land.

Joe had a Clydesdale temperament. He was an unhurried, uncomplicated man, at least at work. Domestically, however, life was much more frantic. The trouble was he couldn't stop breeding. He and his fertile wife produced offspring on an annual basis at about the time

6

of the leek shows – until with a posse of scruffy bairns running about in nothing but short vests, and the latest one sleeping in the bottom drawer of the kitchen press, the parents were apparently advised of the cause, and persuaded to "take precautions".

He claimed he was born in the back of a wagon on the May-Term flittin' day, half way between Elsdon and Alnwick. I can't vouch for that of course, but it is more than likely that several farm workers' children DID enter the world while on the move. It's not so long ago that the local journal had perhaps two full pages of agricultural situations vacant each early spring, as nomadic hands and shepherds shifted from one farm to another, in search of a better cottage, a better boss or an extra shilling.

Meanwhile, back on the ranch, my own job description was "odd laddie". This was the accepted derisory title given to the youngest, greenest member of staff, who worked the odd horse and got all the clarty jobs.

My odd horse was Prince. His name might suggest some degree of nobility, but in fact he was a common bit o' work, who had earlier pulled a Ringtons tea van around Newcastle. Prince was incapable of any real effort (such as hauling a cart uphill) without making the most disgusting noises, and there can be little doubt the atmosphere in the city improved considerably when he moved to Shilbottle.

One of my first jobs as a full-time odd laddie was to lead coal from Shilbottle pit to the steam-driven thresher. Towards the end of the day, with Prince plodding his flatulent way home, and m'self dozing on the cart behind him, I fell off – down among the big flat feet of the horse. The good news was Prince stopped. The bad news was he stopped with one of his big flat feet on my right hand, and for several minutes ignored all suggestions that he might move.

"You've taken long enough," said my father, when we eventually got home in the dusk.

"Well," said I, "the bloody horse stood on m'hand didn't he...? Wouldn't get off!"

Father said nowt, just shook his head, but I think he was never entirely convinced I'd ever become a proper peasant after that.

The Night Hitler Bombed Our Henhouse

ON the fiftieth anniversary of the outbreak of World War Two, the media and all those who could remember, dusted off their memories. Heroes and villians·were resurrected, triumphs and disasters re-lived. It may all seem a long time ago, especially if you weren't born then, perhaps even irrelevant, but for many those war years remain the most dramatic of their lives.

My personal recollections are less than heroic. I was just a country kid then, and down on the farm the war almost passed us by . . . almost.

To be honest we didn't suffer any real hardships. There was food rationing of course, no bananas, no peaches, no chocolate – but farmers could "cure" the occasional pig – and eggs, bagies and potatoes were plentiful enough. What's more the gourmet peasants of North Northumberland were hardly a major threat to the Third Reich, and quite understandably Hitler largely ignored us. Nevertheless for a while we did have an underground shelter in the back field, just in case – until a wayward bullock fell into it one night, and that was the end of that.

Father was the local Air Raid Warden, equipped with dark blue uniform, a tin hat, plus a whistle and a rattle to warn the neighbourhood of any impending attack. I think a central controller somewhere would phone to say German bombers were likely to pass our way (perhaps heading for Glasgow or Wallsend) and a warning should be given. Father would then wander wearily to the farm gate and blow or rattle, whichever was appropriate. Some hours later the controller would phone again to say the danger was past, but by this time Daddy would be tucked up in bed, and as far as I can remember he never got up to give the "all-clear". Indeed there may still be a few nervous folk cowering in their netties for all I know – waiting for a long blast on a whistle.

Then it happened, no warning. Out of a bright starry autumn sky the Luftwaffe attacked our farm.

"Nonsense," I hear you cry, "surely the Nazi hordes were fully engaged in Russia and North Africa, they were desperately trying to control most of Europe, their evil plan for world domination was already beginning to disintegrate. Any suggestion that the German Chiefs of Staff might be sitting in a bunker deep in the Black Forest, conjuring up some fiendish plot to wipe out a farm beside Shilbottle, and so turn the whole course of the war in one terrible night of carnage, is hardly believable . . ."

Well, be that as it may, let me tell you about it. There I was, an innocent peasant child, asleep in my bed one October night in 1942 when all hell broke loose. I was woken by frantic voices and panic activity outside, and peering dozily from the bedroom window, I could see several people running about in their pyjamas or nighties.

"Aha," you say, "I thought as much – one of those secret rural orgies we sometimes read about, some sort of Northumbrian fertility rite perhaps, obscene corn dollies and too much turnip wine . . ."

Not so, it was the Luftwaffe I tell you, and they were bombing us!

I quickly slipped into the ever-ready wellies and ran out into the yard; it was pandemonium. Jack the tractor driver, in calf-length night shirt and steel-toed boots, rushed past carrying two pails of water. Father, who obviously imagined his authority might be threatened if the staff saw him in night attire, had dressed as if for the market, complete with cap and the fancy horned stick he carried everywhere. "What's going on?" he demanded.

"I was just comin' to get y'," spluttered Jack, "y'd better tek cover, women and children forst, t' the shelters, it's the Hun . . ." and with that he staggered off into the darkness.

I followed Father up towards the stackyard where the main activity seemed to be. Sure enough there was trouble. The north side of the hayshed was alight, four stacks of barley were burning, and in the field across the road the hen-house was on fire too.

"Let the bloody hens out," commanded Father, slipping easily into his Kitchener of Khartoum role. "Draw some water from the dipper," he yelled, "beat out the flames on those stacks . . ."

Auld Edith, a toothless biddy from the farm cottages who milked the house cow twice a day, grabbed his sleeve. "It's the Jormins," she cried, "they've invaded, we'll aal be raped i' wor beds..." Even I suspected this was unlikely, and if the silly Jormins had any carnal designs on wor Edith, then they certainly deserved to lose the war.

I bravely opened the hen-house door (the sneck was quite hot) and the relieved Rhode Island Reds scrambled out, some of them with tail feathers smouldering.

However, Edith's assessment of the situation wasn't entirely inaccurate, we were under incendiary attack from the German Air Force. All right then, one of them – somebody actually caught a glimpse of the swastika-ed aeroplane up there in the night sky. I'm led to believe Germans haven't got a great sense of humour (or maybe it's just different) but surely that air crew must have chuckled a little if they could see us. Peasants in pyjamas and cloth caps, womenfolk in nighties and bonnets, all running about in circles with buckets, hay forks, and one knackered stirrup pump – and Father threatening the enemy with his fancy stick. Perhaps they saw him, because they dropped nothing else and flew off home to the Fatherland in triumph.

Back on the ground the situation was almost under control when Tucker Pattinson and his mates came meandering down the road from the Farriers Arms. Naturally they were filled with a proper patriotic fervour (as well as a lot of beer) and without hesitation they proceeded to assist our endeavours, using a method seldom found in any fire brigade manual. Tucker himself, poor chap, got a little too close to the flames, and (or so he claimed) burned a bit of his "fire fighting" equipment. Edith took him away to repair any damage, with a gleam in her eye.

The rest of us went about the stackyard stamping out the last embers, and at about midnight retired to the kitchen to drink tea and compare tales of derring-do. The real fire brigade arrived at one o'clock.

Constable Percival and a man from the Ministry came next day to draw up a report on this dastardly attack. The official explanation was that the German pilot had probably been lost, and having discovered his mistake in the light of the fire and the moon, had gone home, and that seemed reasonable enough.

Nevertheless we all became quite excited about our part in Hitler's downfall, and Edith reckoned we might all get medals. P.C. Percival promised he'd suggest this to Mr Churchill the next time they met, but meanwhile could he keep the semi-barbecued hen he'd found lying in the ditch across the road.

Batman And Robin

HUNTING is an anachronism, feudal, a barbaric sport performed by rural vandals who dress up in fancy costume, climb onto a bewildered horse, blow a trumpet in its ear, and gallop off with a bunch of dim-witted dogs in search of a fox who's usually much cleverer than all of them.

Or, on the other hand, it's a colourful rural pursuit enjoyed by true lovers of the countryside, a bit of olde English heritage still preserved in the face of a shrinking landscape, and ill-informed saboteurs with pockets full of aniseed.

Well it's neither really, it's just a damn silly way to spend a Saturday afternoon. Take my word for it, I've been there. You'd be far better off watching Newcastle United, or even taking the wife shopping at the MetroCentre.

For five or six years I plodged across Northumberland on a superannuated gelding, in the distinguished company of the 7th Percy cavalry. I view-halloo-ed with the best of them. I galloped over other farmers' maiden seeds as if I didn't know what they were. I clattered through neighbours' yards as if I was the landlord. I drank the free whisky offered at the Meet, and generally behaved like a mounted moron.

All to catch a smelly old fox? I hardly ever saw one.

No, it was my old man's idea. You see he was a tenant farmer on the Duke's estate, had been all of his life – and the hope was that when I grew up to be a genuine peasant, I would get a farm too. After all there was no other worthwhile occupation, no other proper jobs. You were either a farmer, or a townie waster with paid holidays and a pension.

The trouble was there weren't plenty farms to go round. The Duke was considered such an enlightened landlord that whenever a place came up to let, a queue of eager applicants quickly formed stretching north into Scotland and south beyond Darlington. To have any chance of getting a tenancy you had to have what was known as "the inside turn".

Now this either meant being in possession of photographic evidence of your granny in a compromising position in the back of a horsebox with an earlier Duke – or joining the huntin' set.

11

Father, sadly realising that the family photos were no use in this instance, decided the best way for young Henry to get ahead was to get him a horse.

He didn't consult me – he just went out, and (no expense spared) paid thirty-five quid for this demented creature who had once come fourth in a hurdle race at Sedgefield. Robin (can you imagine a sillier name for a horse?) was the biggest, evillest equine in England, and his one ambition was to rid himself of the nervous nuisance on his back.

He had two main methods of achieving this. One was to gallop at great speed under very low branches – the other was a little more subtle. You know when you're considering buying a new car, the advertising literature always says "this superb Sierra (or Cavalier or whatever) will go from 0-60 in 8.5 seconds". Well, this horse of mine could go from 60-0 in one second. Of course, I couldn't manage that, and tended to carry on by m'self – between his lugs like Batman. They reckon you can't ride a horse properly until you've fallen off a few times. Well, all I've got to say is if that's the criterion I should've been the best horseman in Europe – but not so.

Nevertheless I was hoisted up onto this "mean machine" and sent forth to impress the aristocracy, and so acquire the tenancy of a farm on the Duke's estate. I have to tell you I never made it. I just didn't have the class, or the style or whatever it takes. You see not only was I never completely

in control of the horse, I didn't dress properly either and it was noticed. Well, money was tight, and there was no striding purposefully into Isaac Walton's ordering jodhpurs, jacket and kinky boots all on Daddy's account. That wasn't part of the deal. He'd bought the transport, the rest was up to me. Consequently I would arrive at some stately home for pre-hunt drinky-poohs in smelly wellies, holey jeans, anorak and an old cloth cap tied on with baler twine lest it blew away in the heat of the chase. Some upper-crust gentleman was heard to remark: "I don't know who the fool is, but he looks and rides like a bloody Mexican bandit."

Be that as it may, Robin and I careered about the county for several years with the Percy. Some days we just stood and froze beside a wood, dripping wet, while the dogs yapped about in rings after a rabbit. Some days we went like the wind over fields and dykes and ditches, as if charging the Russian guns in the valley of death. Sometimes Robin and I stayed together.

It couldn't last, and the climax of our hunting career came on a bleak February morning west of Alnwick. It was then it became apparent that father's master plan wasn't going to work.

On this day the riders, perhaps 40 of them, arrived at a gate in the corner of a field. The hounds had already scrambled through the wire fence in pursuit of their prey, and the huntsmen was anxious to be after them. This gateway, however, was surrounded by an acre lake of clarts, where a herd of cows had stood abluting all winter long. The dark green morass was two feet deep in places, and naturally no one in their right mind was going to gallop carelessly through that.

In such circumstances there is a rule of behaviour, it goes like this. When a group of huntin' folk come to a closed gate, he who bothers to open it shall be allowed through first. The rest will stand patiently by and wait until he completes the operation. The last bloke through is supposed to fasten it again, but that (as some farmers will tell you) is another story.

Anyway, the gentleman who opened this particular gate was duly accorded the aforementioned courtesy. He was a substantial figure not only in the hunting field, but in the wider farming circles as well. In fact he was a man of immense power and influence. He was none other than the agent to the Duke, the power behind the throne, the Ayatollah of the Alnwick area, the man who really decided who had their roof repaired, or their hayshed rebuilt after a storm – and which eager peasant got the tenancy of a farm.

He it was then, this very important aristocrat, who tiptoed his very important aristocratic gee-gee carefully through the mire and opened the gate, while the others stood back in the time-honoured fashion.

It appears no one was aware that at this moment, approaching at the speed of light, was a big evil horse completely out of control, and clinging to it a figure in a cloth cap, wellies and anorak, riding in the unmistakable style of a nervous Mexican bandit.

Robin saw the gate (so conveniently open) saw the other horses lined up (as if in welcome) and roared through the lot, covering them all from head to toe in dark green smelly stuff.

We might've got away with it if the stupid beast had carried on into the middle distance and out of sight, because for a moment or two of course everybody had their eyes shut. But he didn't, no sooner through the gate and onto dry land at the other side, he stopped. He stopped and sniggered.

I can assure you hell hath no fury like an upper-crust posse covered all over in, well . . . call it slurry if you like.

I emigrated to Scot's Gap shortly after that, all hope gone.

Separated By A Common Language

I'VE often envied a natural ability "t' taak proppa". I mean that distinctive brand of upper crust English, associated with the Establishment, the City, and Conservative cheese and wine orgies everywhere.

The outstanding merit of this limb of our language is not only can it open exclusive doors on well oiled hinges, but – provided one's vowels remain nicely rounded, consonants neatly clipped, and the lower orders left totally bewildered – one is seldom required to say anything remotely meaningful.

I first noticed this linguistic gulf twixt them and us at a relatively early age, when well-bred, well-educated, well-heeled teenagers would all conspire to ignore we less favoured brats. Their vocabulary was overloaded with exaggerated adjectives, "absolutely splendid, really soopa, quite stunning . . . " and other ordinary words acquired extra letters; "grarss, clarss, gorn". They "larfed" a lot at what seemed to be singularly unfunny anecdotes. They often rode horses and went "orf" to be successful. Furthermore I discovered any attempt to intrude upon their scintillating conversations was misguided, and only led to embarrassment. They were deaf to a Geordie accent. Even if you announced through a loud hailer that their horse was on fire, the best they'd come up with would be a dismissive smile (and possibly a quick "soopa") before galloping all over you, as if you didn't exist.

Later I discovered my old landlord was similarly afflicted. A charming man from Yorkshire, he nevertheless seemed unable to look a mere peasant in the eye. If, for instance, we were standing in the farm yard, and Cheviot happened to be situated somewhere beyond my left shoulder, he would inform Cheviot that my rent was going up.

When I attempted to attract his attention with forthright argument based on sound agricultural economics, the demands of a growing family, and the 'deed yow' I'd dragged in front of his car – he'd smile benevolently at Cheviot and say something like . . . "splendid, that's settled then . . . really must be orf . . ." and orf he'd jolly well go, presumably to chat with another receptive mountain.

However, having spent my formative years in and around Shilbottle, it was never likely I'd master the smooth cultured confidence of well-spoken feudal folk. Almost inevitably I'd grow up taakin' like the shepherd and m' fithor as I clung to their short tails i' the lambin' field. As it happens I think I'm more or less bilingual now, fluent enough in both languages to translate for the bewildered visitor from abroad or Cheltenham, who finds no mention of 'Haddaway yem' in his pocket phrase book.

One day last summer, when the corn was green and the oil seed rape a dazzling yellow, two friends came to stay for a few days. The couple were from Seattle in the top left hand corner of the United States, and were "doing" Europe – last week, France, this week England.

Well you know how it is when rare visitors fly in from the dark side of the Earth – you have to shut the shop and give them a good time, so, among other things, I took them to Alnwick Castle.

I reckoned Americans particularly would always be interested in a real castle, a touch of live history. It may not be as big as the Grand Canyon, but it's got to beat Disneyland.

And so it proved. They were thrilled. It was "unbelievable, fantastic, so old." They wandered like kids in a chocolate factory through rooms where Canalettos and Turners and long-gone Percys looked down from high stone walls. The furniture, the fireplaces, the ceilings, the armoury fascinated them, and they began to imagine what life in this fortress might've been like hundreds of years ago.

Luckily it was explained to them by a local "expert" who having heard

their excitement felt obliged to contribute his four pennyworth to Anglo-American relations.

"Canny castle eh?" he said looking past them over the battlements towards the river.

"Pardon me?" asked Miss U.S.A.

"Aye them Scots brayed away at this place for donkeys y'knaa . . . " She gave him a charming but bewildered smile.

"'Y' can see the daft buggers," he went on pointing to the north, "'y' can see them teemin' ower the pastures like bumlers an' tryin' t' git ower the waal." He leaned over the parapet and looked down at the imagined kilted hordes . . . "wat a yarkin' they wud git, eh?"

"Of course," she said, without any understanding at all. Our guide, encouraged, leaned confidently on the old stones. "Even if some o' them did manage t' scraffle up," he said, "nee bother, them Porsies ran back inta the keep ower yonder, an' barred that muckle grite door. Plenty bait in there y' knaa, an' a fifty foot hole full o' watta. They just cum oot when they fancied howkin' the Scots sum mare."

The Americans were looking at me for a translation and some relief, so I whisked them away to Warkworth for a bar lunch and another castle.

Next morning they were up early after a restless night fighting with besieged Porsies, and after breakfast we drove up to the mart for a slice of twentieth century farming life. It was another warm dry day. Mother Nature threatening to ease the drought with an occasional cloud over Scots Gap, but with no serious intent.

"Stand on," shouted the auctioneer as we entered the ring, "noo these beast'll shift anywhere, grand sorts . . . luk a' their hint ends . . ."

"Oh my gahd," said the lady from Seattle, "they're at it again – it was easier in France."

The farmer next to me leaned over and in a friendly way, said: "From America are y' hinny? Aye, I've got a dowta in California. She tells us it's aaful droothy ower yonder n' aal. We've had nee rain since the back end y'knaa, nee grass, can hardly mind wat clarts luk like..." He laughed, and so did my guests, but they weren't sure why.

The auctioneer was having trouble selling some young stirks. "Moderate bullocks," advised our agricultural consultant, "y' want nowt t' dee wi' them bonnie lad – they're far ower femmer." Two minutes later they were knocked down to him, and he disappeared after the vendor in search of luck money.

The couple flew back to Seattle convinced Northumberland was an independent state – beautiful landscape, beaches beyond compare, more than its fair share of history, neat and tidy farms, and a language that defied comprehension.

I thought of them a week later, when coming out of a newsagent's in Morpeth I passed a mother scolding her five-year-old son on the pavement. The lad was whingin' on somethin' aaful.

"Wor Trevor," she declared, "y're gittin' nee bullets an' if y' divvent shut yer gob y'll git a right gud hidin' an' w'll gan strite yem . . . !"

Now what would an extra-terrestrial being from the outer galaxy have made of that, I wonder . . . ?

Nowt at aal, I suspect.

And Every Dog His Day

WE once had a dog called Sam, named after an animal who appeared in a western series on television. Our Sam bore little resemblance to the film star, a lean wolfish beast who in each episode would apprehend a renegade Apache or an evil bank robber, and sit slobbering on his chest until Clint Eastwood (or whoever it was) arrived to put the bewildered baddie behind bars.

Our Sam was a "Spanorgi", the result of a brief torrid affair twixt a spaniel dog and a corgi bitch, both from very good homes in Gosforth. He grew up with his father's long body and his mother's short legs, and yet, in spite of these obvious handicaps, devoted his entire life to the defence of our farm against attack from the air. I suspect NATO never knew that we had a dog as clever as their most sophisticated radar. He certainly sensed when an aeroplane was approaching long before anyone else, and would set off as fast as his little legs would carry him, barking his anger at any intruder silly enough to violate our air space. He needed a good start, of course, but throughout his stay with us there were always several well worn tracks over the garden, down the croft, through the barley field, which accurately traced the flight paths of fleeing Phantoms or inter-continental DC10s.

Sam never bothered the farm livestock, and after a while sheep and cattle simply viewed him with bemused indifference as he roared past on his defence mission. By night time he was knackered, and slept fitfully under the kitchen table, perhaps opening one eye occasionally as a jumbo jet at 40,000 feet passed on its way to New York or Tokyo.

Meg was a black labrador who seldom moved at all, at least not with any urgency, unless it was to get at food – any food. She ate anything that was offered or left carelessly within reach – meat, vegetables, high protein sheep nuts, tomatoes, Marmite sandwiches, bananas – everything went down as if sucked into a bottomless vacuum cleaner. A potential burglar would only have to drop a Polo mint to get a free run of the house. When not eating she slept, generally in the missionary position, her fat belly exposed for scratching by passing humans eager to ingratiate themselves with this beautiful seal-like creature. Nevertheless, for her long life she was an integral part of the family, with a distinct sense of humour, able to smile, and almost talk with her big brown eyes. She seemed to love those of us who fed her, and didn't really give a damn about anybody else.

Of course such dogs, no matter how attractive, are of little use to a farmer. They only eat, sleep, fool around, and contribute nowt to the economy. What the stock farmer needs is "a gud collie durg", and such a beast is rare and expensive nowadays.

Shepherds will tell you that there are basically three types of collie. Forget Old English, or Border, or whatever – the breed is not very important. The most mixed-up mongrel can often outperform the purest pedigree, and vice-versa. Fair enough, good parents will often produce a canny pup, but you can't count on it. Generally speaking, it all depends on the relationship between dog and master; both of them need a reasonable degree of gumption. As far as the dog (or durg) is concerned, he or she will usually be classified by the technical farming terms – "useful", "moderate", or "completely donnert".

A donnert collie is best shot at an early age, or at least abandoned somewhere south of Gateshead, otherwise he'll drive his master insane. Many a gentle, carefree auld peasant has been transformed into a foul-mouthed rural fiend by a "donnert durg". The animal may look fantastic – gleaming coat, sparkling eyes, damp shiny nose, a picture fit for "One Man and His Dog" – but this thing will sleep all day hidden among the bales in the hayshed, or he'll be away courtin' with a nymphomaniac terrier from town. He'll never be there when you need him. Tie him up in the byre and he'll howl all night, or eat the door and run off with his girlfriend again. Trouble is he'll come back!

Take him with you to move the yowes and he suddenly becomes deaf. The bright, alert, eager idiot will ignore all commands and chase his tail, pee on a thistle, sit looking intelligent in the middle of the gateway through which you wish the sheep to proceed. Scream at him and he smiles, throw your stick at him and he buries it. There is no solution; the "donnert durg" is a menace. You'll only end up with a sore throat, a heart problem, and a broken marriage.

The "moderate durg" is arguably worse, because you're never quite sure what he'll do. At least the "donnert collie" is consistently useless – this one can be good . . . some days.

"Git away bye, bonnie lad," you shout on Monday, and our canine hero will streak off like a greyhound from trap three, gather the whole flock, fetch them gently "t'hand", and sit there waiting for the next order, keen to please. Brilliant.

"Git away bye, bonnie lad," you say on Tuesday, but this time he will only fetch half the flock, and at the speed of light drive them straight past you through the hedge and into the field beyond. You'll whistle and plead and threaten, jump in and out of your wellies, but to no avail. The next time you see the fool he's got the other half piled three deep in the far corner, and he's grinning, convinced he's Spot the wonder dog.

Give exactly the same instructions on Wednesday, and he'll just sit there as if you'd spoken in some obscure dialect familiar only to the dogs born and bred in Lithuania. This can be very disappointing.

The "useful durg" is brave, intelligent, and expects no more than the occasional compliment, and his supper every night. His only thought is to understand the shepherd's wishes. Naturally there will be the odd breakdown in communications – they won't always speak the same language and, let's face it, the vocabulary of most shepherds is often less than lyrical. But all things considered, the "useful durg" is always worth his weight in chicken liver kennelmeat.

The best collie I ever had was called Sweep. He was fast, fearless, and never took the huff, no matter what I threw at him. He might've been a TV star if he'd had a different master, but the language I used was never suitable for early evening viewing. Nevertheless, Sweep generally understood what was required, and did his best without question.

I recall he and I walking some cattle from Shilbottle to Alnwick mart. The job would be impossible with today's traffic, but then the only real hazard was Tommy Ord's bus. As we approached the narrow bridge over the College Burn, I noticed the fence was broken at the far side. If the cattle got through they'd be off into the wood and disappear, so I ordered the faithful Sweep to go forward and guard the gap. Obeying instantly he leapt over the parapet of the bridge (thinking it was no more than a low wall) and plummeted about 30 feet to the rocky river bed below. He was quite badly injured, and I was obliged to carry him the rest of the way into town.

The vet was confused. "How did this happen?" he asked.

"The dog jumped over the bridge," I said.

"What on earth did he do that for?"

"Well, I suppose because I told him to," I explained.

He gave me one of those special sideways looks that Scottish vets are particularly good at. "I'm not sure you're fit to own a dog," he said.

Spring Lamb

THERE'S a lonnen going south from the farm where townies on weekend safaris occasionally stop to have a picnic, or let their dogs out to sniff a tree. Where young courtin' couples park in gateways and steam up the windows, where older couples get deckchairs out of the boot, unfold the News of the World, and just sit absorbing the natural delights of the Wansbeck Valley Over the dyke sheep may safely graze.

One bright Easter weekend a few years ago I watched an urban expedition, maybe half a dozen of them, disembark from an old Volvo and proceed to grope eagerly about in the hedge. They were armed with plastic bags, and when asked what they were doing their leader calmly replied: ". . . not t' worry mister – w' heard this was a good place for brambles . . ."

Brambles in March!! Was this man from outer space? Or even Killingworth, perhaps?

Of course, as most green, environmentally aware folk will know, March and April in the countryside is not a time for fruit picking – it's the lambing season. That time of year when the yowes of the world conspire to frustrate the shepherd, confound his collie dog, and push both of them into the abyss of madness.

I can't remember, but I expect Killingworth man quickly abandoned his futile bramble search to watch a field of ewes and lambs gambolling in the spring sunshine. He would point at them enthusiastically, call his smiling children over to observe this rural phenomenon, and his wife would inevitably sigh: "aaah . . .", all of them carried away on a cloud of sentimental innocence.

It's about a decade since I did a lambing for real but the scars remain. Not really visible, y' understand, not like old war wounds from the Somme or the World Cup. No, I'm afraid it's the mind that's damaged, and every year about now I spend the odd frantic night chasing a phantom gimmer who is "hanging" an enormous single with swollen head and purple tongue. She just has to be caught and helped, but I never get anywhere near her, only twist the bed into a disaster area, and eventually get up next morning completely knackered.

These annual spring nightmares are usually triggered by some happening the day before. For instance, last week, I was chatting to three peasants for whom March means nothing else but . . . "THE LAMBING." The first fella should have started a fortnight ago but nowt had arrived. "Oh, the buggers

23

are in lamb all right," he said, "but that fancy tup w'bowt at Kelso last back-end missed them first time around – he was just playin' aboot . . .!"

The second bloke was in a hurry. "Canna stop," he said, " . . . they're dropping like flies – four pairs and a three this mornin' already, and two more thinkin' about it . . . gotta go."

"Sounds like a good start," somebody ventured.

"Aye, y' think so?" he said as he moved off . . . "They're not due for ten days yet," – and then anticipating further questions, he added, " . . . randy hogg wi' one stone from next door . . . !"

Shepherd number three had a familiar problem. He wasn't scheduled to begin for a few days either, but the sheep didn't know that. He'd been feeding his pregnant ewes still a full week before "armageddon" when, lo and behold, there in the middle of the frosty field were two little miserable newcomers, alone, ignored, shivering, empty. Whoever was responsible for them obviously wasn't interested, was denying all knowledge, not guilty.

She was somewhere in the crowd of other supposedly devoted mothers, all stuffing their faces at the troughs. Of course, our hero eventually singled out the culprit and caught her, but only to discover she was as lean as a piece of kinlin, and had no more milk than a breeze block. He was fairly philosophical about it all, did what any experienced shepherd would do in such circumstances; he kicked the stupid bitch as hard as he could and limped home to the comfort of the kitchen with the perished pair of lambs tucked under his coat.

The most traumatic lambing I can recall was as a raw callant working for my father. Father must've had some kind of brainstorm that year, or maybe it was all a cunning plot to persuade me to be a solicitor instead of a peasant. Whatever it was, he decided to treble the ewe flock and divide that lambing into three sessions.

First, in February came the Cheviots. Now I doubt if many readers are familiar with Cheviot sheep (chances are they'd be in a rest home for the disturbed by now anyway), but let me tell you that out of the fifty or more varieties of sheep in this country, this one is probably the most lethal. You have to get up very early and be super fit to get the better of these creatures.

Cheviots travel at the speed of light propelled by a constantly revolving tail, and have a wild, demented, terror-stricken glint in their eyes at all times – apparently convinced the shepherd only has designs to slaughter them all. By the time I'd finished lambing a hundred of them they were probably right. I was a decade older and speaking to nobody but m'self.

But that was just the beginning. No sooner had the Cheviots been dealt with than the main flock of Scottish Half-Breds came into the plot. Half-Breds are so called because Daddy was a Border Leicester and Mother was a Cheviot – so arguably they're only half as daft. Certainly they are a lot slower (usually because they're permanently lame) and so easier to catch, yet still with that in-bred talent to drop dead for no apparent reason, or produce triplets while firing on one tit.

And then came the Blackies (Scottish Blackface sheep). I don't know where Father bought these things, but undoubtedly their overriding ambition was to get back there. They seemed to have some low-tech homing device built into the vacant space between their lugs. I never knew where I might find them in the morning. Fences were but a minor irritant, a feeble challenge to crawl through or leap over.

They lambed everywhere except in our lambing field. In someone else's lambing field perhaps, in a thorn bush, in a ditch, on the road – all over the place. Bring them into the cosy confines of the yard at night, and like Arapaho Indians who resent the restrictions of the reservation, they would creep silently away before dawn – heading west into their sacred burial grounds towards Bellingham or wherever.

By the end of April it was all over. The twins were on the maiden seeds, the singles on old grass, the barren yowes cashed, the dead buried, the straw shelters burned – and the inevitable orphans grazing in the garden.

Spring, and not a bramble in sight.

It's All In The Game

SUMMER . . . sounds of willow on leather, seven iron to the green, a lob to the baseline.

Sadly, I've never really been much good at sport, never a likely athlete, plenty enthusiasm but not a lot of talent. Throw a ball or an apple at a natural games player and he'll catch the thing quite effortlessly with one hand. He's probably tying the laces on his trainers at the same time.

"Catch", somebody shouts, and by the time my brain has sent warning messages to a bewildered and unco-ordinated body, I turn, just in time for the apple to hit me between the eyes.

As a youth I played cricket for several summers with a village team in the Alnwick and District 'B' league. My hero in those days was Denis Compton. That's who I wanted to be like, the carefree cricketing cavalier, the lad who turned up just in time to put on his scruffy off-white gear, grab an old bat, and with his cap at a jaunty angle, knock up a quick century before lunch.

Better still, why not an all-rounder? Bowling subtle off-breaks from the Pavilion End on a perfect length, routing the Red Row XI, bamboozling Broomhill. Or swooping in the covers like Neil Harvey, picking up and throwing in one poetic movement, the ball flying like a guided missile, crashing into the stumps leaving the batsman stranded and amazed.

Once while batting against Shilbottle, facing a dark haired demon called Morton, I went down on one knee to sweep the ball Compton-like, gracefully away to fine leg. I missed the damn thing of course and it hit me on the nose. Now it has to be admitted that I already had an above average hooter, but within minutes it had swollen to elephantine proportions and I couldn't see past it. Furthermore, the heartless Morton appealed with such ferocity that the umpire was persuaded to give me out . . . N.B.W. I suppose.

Our team was largely made up of country lads, and one of them, Jimmy, a local shepherd, was a massive bloke, as hard as concrete, indestructible, and he was our wicket keeper. He wasn't particularly mobile, didn't leap about like Alan Knott or Jack Russell, but he was so big standing there in his braces that any ball beating the bat inevitably hit him somewhere, and stopped. He was impervious to pain.

Playing at home to Seahouses I was fielding in a position quite close to the batsman known as silly mid on. This was certainly not because I was particularly brave or possessed lightning reflexes, but rather because I couldn't throw a cricket ball more than about fifteen yards. No good putting me way out on the fence, I might perhaps stop the ball going over the boundary for four, but then I'd have to carry it all the way back to the wicket keeper, by which time the batsmen had probably ambled six.

Anyway there I stood alert at silly mid on, ready for the sharp catch from a faulty stroke – and sure enough it came. The batsman prodded forward to a rising delivery, the ball flew off the shoulder of the bat high into the air halfway between Jimmy and m'self.

"Mine," I shouted.

"No it's mine," said Jimmy.

We met head on long before the ball arrived. He caught it and I was carried off unconscious.

I once thought tennis might have possibilities – no real pretentions to be a Becker y' understand, but like Betjeman I had visions of bright young females with long brown legs emerging from short white skirts flinging themselves about the court with athletic abandon, a host of Joan Hunter-Dunns smiling at me over the net. In fact girls tended to giggle a lot when they caught sight of my ridiculous knees peeping out below baggy shorts. Some of you may know that this can be quite discouraging.

One of the great attractions of golf is that even professionals such as Woosnam, Lyle and Faldo can sometimes be humbled by the game. At the same time ordinary mortals with a handicap of 25 can occasionally, on a really good day, get two pars and a birdie on the trot, and imagine (albeit briefly) that they could take the money from anybody. If ever there was a game that mixed triumph and despair, this is it. It's so simple, all you have to do is hit that little white ball with one of these specially designed clubs, until you've put it into that hole over there. Surely anyone can do that – even arthritic old grannies play. Douglas Bader was pretty good, and he had two tin legs.

Be that as it may, this game can reduce any stout-hearted resolute man, with the constitution of a Clydesdale, to a whimpering mealy-mouthed psychopath capable of stealing sweeties from orphans.

It's all in the head y'see. No matter what Jack Nicklaus might tell you about the grip, the stance, the swing or whatever, if there isn't a perfect tranquillity between your lugs bordering on a vacancy, you can be in trouble.

For instance, did I ever tell you about Arthur? (Actually I've changed his name because I hope to play with the bloke again.) Well, he always had a head full of theories on how to play the game, there wasn't a problem that couldn't be solved by some slight adjustment in technique. We were playing in a four-ball somewhere in Scotland and duly arrived on the 12th tee. Here the fairway ran alongside a caravan site protected reasonably enough by a high mesh fence. When it came to Arthur's turn to drive off he hit a 'screamer' straight through the only hole in this fence. The ball travelled like a bullet no more than six feet from the ground for a distance of about 200 yards between the rows of mobile homes. Fortunately I think it was a rather dull day, and most holidaymakers must've been inside having tea, otherwise the shot could have decapitated several of them.

"That's out of bounds," one of us said, so our man prepared to play again, this time with a slight amendment to the position of the feet perhaps. The second drive went a prodigious distance right down the middle of the fairway – a tremendous shot. Sadly, however, the club slipped out of his hands and took off into a nearby cornfield. The sight of a golfer looking for a lost ball may not be unusual – a golfer searching for a wayward driver is somewhat rarer.

I still believe he created some sort of golfing history on the 16th tee at Morpeth. The party who were lucky enough to be present on that day must realise they were privileged.

On this occasion our hero prepared to drive with his usual careful routine (everybody has one) . . . relax, swing slowly. The Whalton road looms menacingly on the left, but otherwise no real problems . . . unless of course your brain is playing a video of Seve thrashing a majestic shot over 300 yards of water at Augusta . . .

Anyway, whatever it was, something went wrong with Arthur's plan somewhere in mid-swing. He managed to hit the ball all right, but it flew off the tee peg directly up his left trouser leg.

Luckily it didn't get too far, or it might've been the end of what I believe is still a promising sporting career . . .

Rural Pursuit

THE only evidence was a trail of dog biscuits leading out of the field, through the gateway and out onto the road, where tyre marks on the verge indicated that a vehicle had been parked there during the night.

What's been going on? A courting couple perhaps with a self-conscious labrador who'd been too embarrassed to watch and gone for a walk, got lost in the dark . . . ? Wrong.

Well, how about a coven of Wansbeck witches high on dandelion wine and liver-flavoured Kennomeat . . . satanic shenanigans . . . some kind of rural Geordie Orgy? No, the parish council wouldn't stand for that!

Ram raiders maybe. The Hole in the Wall Gang, fresh from a carefree evening's work at the crash 'n' carry, sharing out their haul in the middle of a field? Not quite, but you're getting warmer . . . give in?

All right I'll tell y' – it was rustlers! Seems these villains had tried (unsuccessfully) to tempt a flock of nervous Cheviot ewes out of the field and into a waiting van. I suspect the owner of the sheep might've been delighted to see the back of them, but the awkward things wouldn't go. Cheviots are like that.

There's nowt new about this crime, of course. Men have been stealing sheep for years, and several of today's aristocracy might well attribute their current position to a few fruitful forays over the fence, or over the border, by their rotten reivering ancestors.

In those days, you may remember, it was considered very naughty indeed, and rustlers unlucky enough to be caught were hanged from a gibbet until they were thoroughly convinced of their folly, and in no condition to do it again.

Nowadays it is more likely that the sentence will be suspended, rather than the wretched rustler. Furthermore, serious though the crime undoubtedly is, a suspicion remains that rustling may still be viewed as some kind of "romantic" villainy.

Suburban burglary is common enough, but sheep stealing in the dead of night up the Coquet valley, or wherever, might conjure up some ridiculous delusion of a Robin Hood figure, or Billy the Kid, in the mixed-up mind of an adventurous townie thief. But I wonder if they know what they're letting themselves in for. I wonder how many sorties end in frustration and despair for want of proper research and rural know-how.

For instance, we might well imagine a pair of entrepreneurial townie robbers, already with a garage full of "hot" microwaves, deciding that a spot of sheep stealing could be an interesting variation, and an easy way to supplement the dole. So, dressed darkly, faces blacked, carrying a bag of dog biscuits, and accompanied by the inevitable lurcher, our heroes set off into the dark blue night in their dark blue Transit, in search of instant mutton take-away. The country lanes are deserted, country folk are abed, the rural world is still. Quietly they park in a remote gateway, switch off the lights, and tiptoe into the field. The clever plot is to attract the innocent sheep to the troughs, and grab a couple of them as they're feeding. Simple enough: sheep aren't supposed to be very bright.

Little do they realise, however, that their intended victims in this exercise are the infamous "lean mule yow" variety, a permanently ravenous breed of sheep, capable of destroying even the most experienced shepherd, and before you can say "git away bye", our two braves are completely overwhelmed in the rush, trampled into the clarts, and the biscuits consumed in a trice. The poor lurcher flees in terror; he's never seen anything like these creatures before, and within seconds the sheep are out through the gate and away up the road into a field of wheat. Perhaps one of the rustlers might make a despairing grab at the last yow. She's obviously very old, lame, and coughing a lot – surely at least she can be caught. But all he's left with is a handful of wool as she contemptuously sidesteps past him into the inky darkness. This is not at all how the lads imagined it would be, and pride demands they try again. It will be dawn soon, and they feel obliged to pinch something before they go home to Mafeking Gardens.

"Why don't we rustle some cattle?" asks one of them. "I remember seeing Lee Marvin do it once, looked fairly easy. All y' do is grab one while it's asleep and gallop off into the hills . . ."

"Well, all right," says his mate. "Just one then, and a little un'll do nicely. After those sheep I reckon nickin' videos is a canny bit safer."

Up the lane they come across a slumbering herd lying dreamily chewing the cud in thin moonlight. Rather nervously they climb over the fence and creep silently like Apaches in amongst the cattle. The cattle don't seem to care, the odd beast opens an eye and views the intruders with detached boredom, but nothing moves. This looks much more promising.

30

"Here's a small black one," whispers the chief rustler. "Let's grab it and get t'hell outa here." (He's even beginning to sound like a rustler.)

It takes this dozing calf about three seconds to wake up and realise that some idiot is pulling on his tail – at which point the bewildered animal calls for mother – and mother, a hairy cross Galloway psychopath of uncertain age, moves with the speed of a missile. She emerges out of the gloom bellowing and snorting and slavering like some monster from the Black Lagoon, followed closely by all the other concerned mothers. The noise is horrendous, the panic instant!

Lee Marvin quickly lets go of the calf's tail and flees with his buddy. They take the fence in one Olympian leap as the whole herd crashes through in an unstoppable stampede. The unfortunate lurcher, who has wisely observed this terror from the half opened window of the van, now tries desperately to retreat further and hide in the glove compartment, as the rusty old vehicle is totally wrecked about his ears.

The poor rustlers are forced to abandon everything, and eventually limp home bruised and battered and covered in muck, convinced they must have accidentally stumbled into some sort of wild game reserve.

Next morning a farmer finds his sheep lying as full as eggs on his neighbour's wheat, while his neighbour's cows and calves are happily grazing among the headstones in the village churchyard.

Back in Mafeking Gardens two blokes with a garage full of microwaves are discussing how to rob the Co-op. A distressed lurcher trembles uncontrollably behind the sofa.

A Farewell To Farms

THERE is a farm somewhere in Northumberland where nothing agricultural ever happens. A farm where no husbandry is practised, no crops are growing. There are buttercups and bindweed of course, but no barley; woodrush and willow herb, but no wheat. The grey-green fields are not grazed by cows and calves or ewes and lambs.

The old fescues, dogstail and Yorkshire fog prosper among rampant thistles, whose seeds float about the parish like gentle summer snowflakes. The hedgerows grow aimlessly, uncut, thin wayward hawthorns meandering from field to field. It may be paradise for a billion butterflies, bugs and beetles, home to a million mice and moles, a retreat for a regiment of randy rabbits, but from a farming point of view, it's nothing but a mess – a waste of space.

At the top of the lane, the byre, the barn and the stable shelter only spuggies and spiders now, and the inevitable collar dove. The sheep pens are overgrown, full of nettles. The old stone farmhouse stands silently staring south. No smells of supper, no chattering children, no grumbling grown-ups, no collie dog patiently dreaming at the back door. Only gossiping ghosts perhaps. A sad, abandoned place, a sort of land-locked Marie Celeste.

Long ago my great great uncle Samuel farmed there, and if perchance you hear a rumbling, rattling disturbance coming from the nearby churchyard, it's probably the man's bones revolving in his grave. How could his old farm be empty? Does no-one want it?

"Ah but wait a minute, hang on," someone cries, "this must be a marvellous place, a perfect place, a heaven on earth. This is how the new green de-chemicalised organic countryside is meant to be, isn't it? Just like the good old rural world once was. A natural wilderness for wildlife, and nice environmentally aware people – like me. Where is this beautiful neglected idyll, where no nitrates, insecticides, herbicides and fungicides drift o'er the flora? Take me there immediately, I want to walk on it, sit on it, play on it, protect it forever!"

"Y'must be joking," another voice pipes up, "t'hell with protecting it – what about that lovely big farmhouse, and all those other antiquated eighteenth century buildings full of character and country charm? What a challenge, couldn't we develop them, re-vitalise them? We would do it very tastefully of course – natural stone is such an attractive material. We could

CLARTIEHOLE FARM
FOR SALE
GREAT DEVELOPMENT
POTENTIAL
EXECUTIVE COUNTRY
HOMES

make a special feature of those quaint old arches, expose the cobbled yard, move the old pump over here. I can see it clearly now – three, maybe four executive homes, all with en-suite facilities, hi-tech kitchens, small garden, patio and pony paddock (I beg your pardon – pony garth). We might even dam the stream. Good lord, a trout lake perhaps . . . how exciting: we could all be millionaires overnight!"

But what about the land, all those empty fields?

"Heavens, almost forgot the land. Memo: phone Peter Alliss tomorrow – question: how many acres do we need for a golf course? A Country Club perhaps . . . ?"

Steady, steady – canny on lads – what's all this about a natural wilderness, executive dwellings, a ruddy golf course? Isn't this supposed to be a place where somebody produces food – beef, eggs, mutton, potatoes, milk or whatever? Isn't that how it's been for a thousand years, stewarded by some awkward auld codger (like my great, great uncle Samuel) who knew how to manage the crops and the livestock, all of it, tidy and cared for? Is that sort of fellow suddenly redundant? Well maybe he is. Maybe there's no room for such a romantic wee figure anymore. Maybe he just has to be written out of the script (like the little corner baccie shop).

The particular farm we're talking about was abandoned for reasons unknown to me, but in any case there's barely a living to be made there now. It's probably too small, not a viable unit, not enough agricultural options to play with. Some of us may think that's rather sad, but whether we like it or not the entire landscape is changing all the time. People move, the city grows, the countryside shrinks, and clever computers conjure new accounts. Fewer and bigger farms husbanded by a handful of bucolic tycoons, a pastoral quilt with bigger squares. A developer's delight – old stables into stately homes, byres into bungalows. Blame world economics, the EEC, the Hip and Thigh diet, mad cows, or rich lawyers in search of a home with a view and character, the fancy 4 x 4 and a BMW parked in the yard. After a fat-free breakfast, he can drive from Clartiehole Farm (through the tarted up village) to the city office in no more than forty frantic minutes. Success. Progress. Perhaps.

Which reminds me . . . we'd been discussing this changing country scene, sadly reflecting on the problems of British agriculture, and some possible reasons for it, when a farmer from the Borders told us this cautionary tale.

It seems he was checking his livestock one Sunday evening, and his gentle stroll took him past a particularly posh new residence on the edge of the village. The lady of the house was pottering about in the garden, and the farmer paused to compliment her on a fine display of fruit and veg. It all looked splendidly productive. Well tended rows of taties, onions, leeks, cauliflowers and cabbages. And beyond there were rasps, tomato plants, strawberries, blackcurrant and gooseberry bushes. This was an impressive show, and he told her so.

"Well thank you," said the lady from the other side of the fence. "Actually we devote a lot of time and effort to our garden now. Angus and I virtually live from it. We grow almost everything we need, and of course we don't eat meat at all . . . !" She declared this with the superior smile of the converted, the enlightened. "Well, it's simply not good for you, is it?" she said. "In fact we've become devout vegetarians – so much better for everyone really – we feel it ensures a longer, healthier life – don't you agree?"

"Aye well, I wouldn't know about that," said our farmer friend quietly. "All I can tell you is I've got about a thousand sheep up there on the hill – and it seems t'me an aaful lot o' them drop dead lang afore their time – and they're all vegetarians!"

With that, I suspect, he bade her a polite good evening, called his collie dog t'heel, and went home for a cold beef sandwich.

34

A Deep Depression

GLADYS was kneeling by the Aga, patiently spooning warm milk, mixed with a little whisky, into the cold mouth of an abandoned triplet. Another orphan lamb had recovered enough to escape from the cardboard box, and stood quietly piddling on the cleaky mat. Sep made a mental note not to eat any biscuits he might drop there . . . better to leave them for the dog – Sweep wasn't so fussy.

"We'll have to fetch the yowes inside t'night," he muttered, "the forecast's bad." And without waiting for any response, he fastened the baler twine around his coat, and went out into the weather.

He knew instinctively where the sheep would be. Some novice peasant might imagine they'd be sheltering behind a hedge or a wall, or better still close to the hayshed away from the wind and sleet. Sep knew better, and sure enough the ewes were all huddled together in the bleakest spot they could find, about to settle down for the night, probably after drawing lots to decide who would have the privilege of dying of exposure before the morning.

The wet was beginning to run down inside his collar, even under leggings his knees felt damp, and the hand that held the stick was almost numb. The sheep seemed numb as well; they would hardly move unless kicked, cajoled and cursed. "The wetter they are the stupider they are," Sep grumbled, as Sweep scuttled back and forth, occasionally nipping a back leg to hurry them up. They were usually persuaded by anything that looked remotely like food, but not tonight. Normally if Sep made a noise like a bale of hay they'd follow him anywhere. Wave an empty bag at them, and you'd probably be trampled into the clarts. Tonight they were being awkward. Sheep are like that sometimes.

So it was a slow, frustrating job, nearly dark already, and trying hard to snow. Perhaps it was the cold, miserable mood he was in that encouraged Sep's mind to wander. He thought of that chap on Scott's disastrous Antarctic expedition, and imagined himself bidding a brave farewell to Gladys, "I'm away to bring the yowes in," he'd say quietly, "I may be gone for some time . . ."

He wondered if anybody else was out and about on a night like this. Certainly most townies would be watching Eastenders, on to their second gin and tonic, and exchanging "darlings" with each other.

"Had a good day at the office, darling?"

"Yes thank you, darling – and you?"

"Oh the children were impossible, darling. And Sainsbury's was absolutely appalling, darling . . ."

The cynical little daydream was interrupted by a bloody-minded mule who tried to bolt back past Sweep. Sep almost shouted "git away bye darling . . . !" but pulled himself together just in time.

Of course there would be other shepherds out tonight doing the same sort of thing, and that made him feel a little better. Charlie next door for instance – except he'd be in a tractor cab with the heater on, screaming obscenities out of the window at his useless dog. he never walked anywhere, and when the ground was dry enough he even shepherded from the front seat of an old Ford van. He toured about the lambing field like Rommel the Desert Fox reviewing his troops before the big battle. He'd removed the driver's door so that when he came upon a sheep in a spot of bother, he could cruise quietly up alongside the unsuspecting beast, and leaning out of the cab as far as he could, grab the animal. Then he'd stop the van and deal with the problem.

It didn't work every time. Sep remembered the occasion a few years ago when Charlie's mobile midwifery came unstuck. He'd been roaring about the field in bottom gear most of the morning, trying to catch a particularly unco-operative gimmer with a devastating body swerve. Again and again he almost caught her, but each time the best he got was a handful of wool. By ten o'clock she looked as though she'd been savaged by a pack of toothless Rottweilers. Then disaster. Charlie was becoming very upset, the elusive bitch simply had to be captured and lambed as soon as possible. He was driving faster and faster, tighter and tighter turns, the still country air filled with darker and darker threats. He almost had a back leg . . . if she'd only run straight for a few yards it would be easy. He couldn't give up now, it was a question of pride. He wouldn't be beaten by a stupid sheep – not him!

The crash was heard throughout the village as Charlie's old Ford went smack bang into the only telegraph pole in the twenty-acre field. The van stopped very quickly, but Charlie, who'd been halfway out of the door carried on for several yards. The gimmer, having at last shaken off this mad screaming predator, promptly lay down and gave birth to twins.

Meanwhile back in the real world Gladys had donned duffle coat and wellies, and was waiting in the yard when Sep and Sweep eventually came in with the ewes. It was dark now, and she'd switched on the hemmel lights. It looked warm, dry, clean and inviting in there – but the sheep wouldn't go in. They stood stubbornly outside in the sleet, their backs to the open shed. Sep grabbed a hurdle, swore and waved his stick, Sweep darted back and forth barking every time his master cursed. The flock stared blankly at the frantic antics of man and dog. Occasionally a ewe would decide to make a dash for freedom back to the field, and only a

36

desperate clout across her nose or a quick nip from the dog would change her mind. Gladys, determined nothing would pass while she lived, threatened any defector with a broom.

Then suddenly it all happened. One of the sheep, perhaps bored by the whole noisy pantomime, just wandered nonchalantly into the hemmel, and the rest followed . . . all except one. She had been eyeballing Sweep at the time and failed to notice the general retreat behind her. Now she looked round to find herself all alone, and panicked. She made to dart past Sep and off into the night, but with lightning reflexes Sep threw the hurdle at the ewe's head, and just in time she turned back to join her companions. The hurdle, however, having been thrown with considerable venom, continued its journey across the yard, and smashed into the car standing at the back door. Sep blamed the ewe of course, and for a moment he considered singling her out so that he could jump on her and kick her to death. Instead he threw his stick at the dog. Sweep, who'd seen this kind of behaviour many times, dodged easily, and retired to the byre to lick himself dry.

Gladys secured the hemmel gate, picked up the stick and handed it to her husband. She did not say "have you had a nice day, darling?" – and he said nowt either. Back in the house the two pet lambs had piddled their way along the passage, and were lying in front of the telly, apparently watching the weather forecast. Ian MacCaskill, with a twinkle in his eye, promised a deepening depression for tomorrow.

TODAYS
WEATHER

Market Forces

HAVE you ever been to an auction mart? No, I don't mean sitting in the sophisticated surroundings of Sotheby's waiting anxiously to flog your Canaletto or a Constable. Nor even a crowded Saturday afternoon spent at the High Street salerooms, bidding for a couch, a commode, or a grandfather clock . . .

I'm talking about "the mart" – that traditional agricultural theatre, where yowes 'n' cows 'n' sows are bought and sold every week, where peasants swap exaggerations, and complain about the government, the EEC, the weather, and the pigeons eating their barley. A place of "shit and sawdust", where men go about their business wearing boots made in Rothbury, and permanently attached to stout sticks.

The first mart I ever attended was in Alnwick. As a youth, Sweep the wonder dog and I would walk fat cattle to the grading every Monday morning, and fetch lean Irish heifers back from the store sale on Friday afternoons.

Most of the feeding cattle came from Ireland in those days, ferried over by Messrs Gormley and McGill, Kelly and McCafferty, Duffy and Dillon – desperate dealers, who every week protested they were makin' nuthin'.

"Ah sweet Jaisus," they would cry to the auctioneer, "Oi cannot possibly sell at that proice – oi'll be loosin' a bloody fortune!"

Mr Thornton, the man in the white coat, would knock them down anyway, to a farmer who thought they were quite dear enough.

Later I made the awful pilgrimage to Gateshead – the coldest, wettest, darkest mart on the face of the earth – a Siberian sale situated in a windswept wilderness just south of the Tyne, where rain fell as soggy soot. Why did simple country folk go to such a perishing place?

Well, I'll tell you . . . because you could sell anything there. If someone turned up with a three-humped camel, there'd be a buyer at Gateshead. Push an old arthritic cow into the ring, a redundant ram, a superannuated sow . . . and you'd always get a bid. The good, the bad and the ridiculous, all sold at Gateshead.

There was a coven of sinister wheeler-dealers there, who wore heavy black coats, and dark trilby hats pulled well down over their narrow eyes. As soon as they'd bought the cow (or whatever) they'd dispatch a rat-like hit man, who scurried away to extract "luck money" before the vendor could flee the premises. There was no way out alive, you had to pay the exit fee . . . the Gateshead mafia saw to that.

38

The first cattle I ever purchased were at Bellingham – a mart where wild and wily hill men crept down from the fells once a year, to confound the naive lowland farmer looking for well-bred livestock to fatten on richer pastures. This naive lowland farmer bought half a dozen cross-Galloway beasts . . . mad, black hairy things, with big lugs and startled expressions. "They'll grow like mushrooms," I was assured. "You'll not recognise them in a couple o' months."

He was right on the second point. Maybe it was the damp weather that winter, but they definitely shrank, and by the following spring looked like nervous pot-bellied spaniels. On reflection, there was never much chance they'd prosper anyway, because the little black divils wouldn't stand still long enough to graze. We eventually sold them at Hexham. I told the bloke who bought them he wouldn't recognise them in a couple of months.

For some farmers, those who grow only cereals, potatoes and such things, marts are of little interest of course. They are just draughty, boring, old-fashioned institutions, where auctioneers gabble a foreign language to a privileged clientele. It's almost an exclusive club, where strangers are viewed with extravagant suspicion. Women (especially pretty women) are often treated like beings from outer space, from Jupiter – or Surrey.

I recall a smart young lady appearing at Scot's Gap mart one Wednesday, years ago. She was selling lambs there for the first time, and appeared in high-heeled boots, a small T-shirt, and very tight jeans. Her fingernails were scarlet. The battle-weary regulars sniggered like teenagers. Smelly, toothless old shepherds were transformed into rural Romeos, and invited her to an intimate beef sandwich in the canteen. The government grader, who was never known to smile at anybody, lest it be misconstrued as some kind of favouritism, beamed and grinned, and said her consignment was "tremendous". The posse of dour wholesale butchers even bid against each other, while staring at her chest, and made no mention of luck money as she shimmied from the ring. The auctioneer almost fell out of his box to take her hand, and ask if she could bring some more sheep next week. There was a delay after she'd gone while he coughed and blew his nose, and pulled himself together, but even then his voice didn't sound right, and he knocked the next lot down far too quickly. At least one old codger wasn't amused. "She shouldn't turn up here looking like Marilyn Monroe," he said. "The lads just lose their concentration. It can ruin the whole trade . . . !"

Another farmer I know was once persuaded to take a lady to buy sheep at the mart. She was a townie lass who had recently acquired a field, and didn't know what to do with it.

"You'll have to keep the grass down," Willie told her. "I'll buy some ewes and lambs for y' . . ."

But that wasn't good enough – she wanted to go to the sale and do the job herself. It was a new adventure. All she needed from Willie was advice on what the creatures were worth.

Standing at the ringside in her Barbour coat, she could hardly contain herself as several lots came and went. Eventually, when a pen of good three crop mule ewes with twins came in. Willie whispered, "these are just what y' need; go on, give him a bid . . ."

The proceedings promptly shuddered to a halt, as the deranged woman leapt up and down, waving her catalogue in the air. Even the sheep stopped and stared at her – then fled to the other side of the ring.

"What the hell are y' doin'?" snarled Willie, disappearing deep into his coat.

"I was only trying to attract the auctioneer's attention," she said. "He might miss me . . ."

"You're jokin'," he said. "The man'll see y' alright, just give him a nod, move a finger, wink at 'im."

"I certainly have no intention of winking at the gentleman," she snorted indignantly. "He might get entirely the wrong impression."

Willie told her not to be so bloody conceited. "All he's interested in is sellin' sheep for as much as possible, and if he finds a crazy woman like you flailin' about as if you were drownin', he'll be thrilled t' bits. You could end up buyin' the entire mart!"

After that madam settled down, barely breathed, moved nothing, only a cautious sideways glance whenever Willie gave her a gentle prod in the ribs. "They're plenty," he'd mutter. "Don't give him any more . . . reckon he's been takin' y' twice anyway."

"You're out on the left," shouts the auctioneer. "Are you bidding? Last chance . . ."

"Ignore 'im," says Willie. "Take no notice . . ."

Three lots later and another prod. "Go on," he whispers. "Give him a quid, but take your time, and don't look so desperately keen . . ."

The man in the white coat seemed to hang on forever before the hammer finally fell, and the lady had her first farming purchase. She gave a little squeal of delight and turned as if to hug her consultant, but Willie had already fled to the mart canteen. It was all becoming a wee bit embarrassing. Some of his mates were giggling as he hurried by.

She found him sitting at a corner table with three other farmers. They had both hands round mugs of dark tea, deep in conversation. The chatter stopped abruptly as she approached, still aglow with her triumph, and clutching a crumpled fiver in her small hand. One old gadgie began to stand up for the lady, but only got half way, before he quickly sat down again when Willie gave him a serious look.

"I see y' got some luck," Willie said. "Well, you'll need a wagon to take them home of course, and a whole lot o' stuff from the vet to inject them, and some ewe and lamb mixture from the store, and maybe a spade." But he stopped there. "Aye, your problems have only just begun, bonnie lass . . ."

The Farmer's Shilling

I HAVE before me The Last Will and Testament of someone who describes himself as "a yeoman of Thropple in the County of Northumberland".

The flawless copper-plate document is signed in a rather shaky hand, but quite legible nevertheless, and witnessed by Messrs William Westgarth and Henry Nixon of Morpeth, on the 19th day of November 1739.

This yeoman admits to being "weak in body but of sound and perfect mind", as he dictates the dispersal of his worldly goods, possibly as he lay a-bed, for alas – he expired a few weeks later at the age of 75.

"I give and bequeath unto my son Joseph," he decrees, "the sum of one shilling, to be paid him within 12 months of my decease."

What's this, for Heaven's sake? A shilling, a measly 12 pence piece, and maybe a year before it's delivered! Is this some kind of cynical joke?

What on earth would a shilling buy then, I wonder: supper for four at the Queen's Head with a flagon of ale perhaps? (I have another scrap of rural history from about the same time which records: "To a man mowing weeds, seven days for eight pence"). So obviously it was unlikely to dramatically change anybody's lifestyle.

However, the old man's magnanimity doesn't end there. "I give and bequeath unto my son Robert," he declares, "the sum of (you've guessed it) one shilling to be paid him within 12 months of my decease."

Another brother, Thomas, receives "the like sum of one shilling," with the same one-year deadline.

At this point I'm beginning to conjure up a picture (just a flight of fancy, you understand) of the entire family breathlessly assembled round the big kitchen table in Thropple farmhouse. Lots of serious rustic faces, all suitably saddened and respectful, stoically determined to mask dismay or delight, as Mr Westgarth, the solicitor, reveals more princely bequests.

It would be a large gathering; Samuel the yeoman fathered at least 10 children we know of, and seven are still alive and well, and (let us suppose) here in the kitchen.

Joseph, the eldest son, already a silver shilling richer, sits grimly unimpressed in his late father's favourite chair by the fire. He hasn't bothered to change out of his working gear, save to remove clarty boots and leggings at the back door – and still smells distinctly of sheep.

His plump wee wife Alice (née Todd of Newton Park, a neighbouring farm just down the lane) and of only marginally sweeter fragrance, stands behind muttering again and again: "A shilling . . . one bloody shilling . . . I don't believe it!"

Brother Robert, married to Alice's sister, doesn't appear to be over the moon either, and glowering at Mr Westgarth as if the man might be party to a fiendish legal conspiracy, stumbles outside to relieve himself in the byre.

Thomas, who is here with his missus, Mary Moor of Mitford, erupts into a fit of coughing and spluttering as his meagre legacy is announced, and Mary vigorously rubs his back, mumbling sympathetic noises, well aware her man could be in a dour fettle for several days.

Eldest daughter Margaret (she who married John Wilkinson of Morpeth) has taken on the catering duties for the occasion, and her busy black figure bustles about the house where she was born, dispensing whisky for the menfolk, tea and scones for the rest of the family.

She is a woman who seldom reveals what she might be thinking, usually a rather stern business-like expression, but today there's just the merest suspicion of a smile hovering about her thin lips. What game is this the old devil's playing, she wonders. A single silver coin for each of her big brothers. What more has he in store?

Some of the others are now finding it difficult not to fidget. Three down and four to go. There's surely some money somewhere, isn't there? The kitchen is as quiet as a frosty night now. Even the two skinny whippets under the table know when to say nowt.

Mr Westgarth, spectacles perched on the end of his nose, seemingly oblivious to the strained atmosphere, his voice still steady and even, takes a sip from his glass and reads on. "To Margaret Wilkinson," he glances up briefly towards her, "the like sum of one shilling to be paid within 12 months of my decease."

Margaret almost drops her teapot and utters the faintest of squeaks, but quickly pulls herself together.

With only a moment's pause, Westgarth carries on. "I give and bequeath unto my granddaughter Jane Shotten" (Ah, a bonnie young favourite here, perhaps – someone who comforted the old man in his dotage maybe?). But no: just another paltry silver coin for Miss Shotten, poor lass.

The lawyer (who is almost certainly enjoying himself) draws a deep breath and proceeds: "To my daughter Mary Robinson, the sum of . . ." (wait for it) ". . . FOUR POUNDS of good and lawful money of Great Britain, to be paid within TWO years of my decease."

Well now, how about that? There must be a reason for this burst of generosity, but no clues. perhaps she was a widow already and needed a little help. Whatever the explanation, Mary is quite overwhelmed. She

43

giggles a little too loudly, and the youngest son George, the last in line, sitting quietly on a stool by the hearth, can barely wait for the next and final pronouncement, though I suspect by now he has a fair idea what it will be.

Mr Westgarth reads this paragraph with much greater deliberation. "And as to all the rest and residue of my personal estate whatsoever," he declares, "I give and bequeath unto my son George, nominating and appointing him sole executor, he paying all my debts and funeral expenses."

So that's it then. The lawyer folds his papers, drains his glass, shakes hands with everyone and rides off back to Morpeth, leaving the family to pick on the bones.

Of course, exactly what George inherited can only be guesswork. There doesn't appear to have been much cash about. In fact, perhaps none at all, hence the one or two-year delay before payment. It was probably up to George to find the money and settle the bequests out of farm income.

However, it's reasonable to assume Thropple was a going concern, with a flock of miscellaneous sheep, a couple of house cows, ducks, geese and some speckled hens. There would likely be a pig to kill and cure every year, some Longhorn cattle grazing by the river, a few acres of thistly barley perhaps, together with assorted implements and hand tools.

The farm would have at least a pair of horses to take people and produce into town, oxen to pull the plough, a temperamental collie or two and, I daresay, a whole lot of rabbits and other game scuttling about in the woods.

All in all, I suspect there was a canny living to be made here. Indeed there must've been: the farm had paid the rent and supported a sizeable clan for several generations. And now old Samuel had decreed his youngest son George should carry on, and take over the husbandry of the place.

That deceased yeoman, he with but a handful of coins, and the necessary fiscal circumspection of a peasant farmer, was my great (times five) grandfather.

It would be interesting to know more of the man and his life, but there's not a lot to go on. Obviously he could read and write, sign his name. For several years he was a churchwarden at St Mary Magdalene, Mitford, so presumably he was a respected citizen of the parish.

He was born in 1665, about the time of the Plague and the Great Fire of London. I don't imagine Samuel ever travelled as far as London, probably had no wish to. King Charles II was prancing about town in '65, but by the time Sam's will was read four other sovereigns had come and gone.

The second George was on the throne, Walpole was Prime Minister and Bonnie Prince Charlie was plotting rebellion. Was this yeoman aware of these famous figures, or were they little more than mythical beings in a far-off land, somewhere beyond the Wansbeck?

Chances are he had enough to concern him at Thropple anyway. His wife Jane had died long before him at the age of 42, while giving birth to stillborn twin girls.

The couple had earlier lost a boy at birth, so even if he didn't leave a fortune, he hadn't done so badly to raise seven kids in hard times.

Of the three older lads, Joseph had settled at Newton Park. Thomas was at Whitehouse Farm, Stannington (paying £54 a year rent to the Earl of Carlisle) and Robert had the tenancy of the nearby Dovecote Farm (same landlord).

This would suggest Samuel had already set up these young men, helped to get them started and maybe given sizeable dowries to his married daughters as well. Perhaps other than the stock on Thropple, and a few shillings under the bed, he had already disposed of his modest wealth.

I think his children really had little cause to complain as Samuel took his leave. What's more, all four sons (now established on their own farms) were about to be players in an agricultural revolution, as the population grew apace, and needed to be fed.

History would suggest leaner and more turbulent times for the earlier tenants of the farm. While Samuel's father Thomas was in charge there was a civil war and the poor King lost his head.

Thomas's father Robert may have seen King James ride south from Edinburgh to succeed Elizabeth, and heard tales of a Yorkshireman called Fawkes who tried to blow up Parliament.

Before that, Samuel's great-grandfather somehow survived the lawless years of the Border Reivers. I wonder, did the Elliots, the Kerrs or the Douglases come galloping out of the Cheviots to swoop on Thropple on dark nights, to steal a few cattle and ravish the womenfolk?

Four hundred years ago the livin' in Northumberland wasn't easy . . . But the farm is still there.

A Suit For All Seasons

HE was obviously an extremely worried man. Not at all the suave confident fellow one remembered. The poor soul just sat there ashen-faced, nervously fidgeting with an empty coffee cup, eyes glazed, staring blankly into the middle distance at nothing in particular.

He was a man about to go over the top into no-man's land and almost certain oblivion. We half expected the miserable wretch to start smoking again at any moment. He was probably hitting the bottle already.

"It's quite terrifying," he stammered, his voice several octaves higher than usual. "Costing an absolute fortune. There seems no end to it. May not survive the ordeal . . . Ruined . . . Never realised it would be like this . . . !"

"Don't be daft," somebody said. "You'll enjoy it man."

"Enjoy it? Enjoy it? You have no idea," sobbed the condemned man. "You don't know what you're talking about. YOU haven't got a daughter about to get married, have you? I'm telling y' the whole thing's totally out of control.

"This is serious show business now, y' know. There's gonna be a cast of thousands. All those bloody awful relations we never speak to – the new in-laws from somewhere south of Darlington – the reception – the stress, the cake, the money, the frocks . . . It just goes on and on and on!"

"Women don't wear frocks any more," muttered a sophisticated bloke from the posh end of Netherwitton. "Dresses, gowns, creations perhaps – but not frocks. Thing o' the past, frocks."

"And then there's the HAT!" the poor chap exclaimed. "The wife's gotta have a fancy new hat to match the new frock!"

"New outfit," suggested Netherwitton patiently.

But the victim wasn't listening. "There are hundreds of strange women ringing up every night wondering what colour this bloody hat is gonna be!" he blubbered. "I told the missus, 'that bonnie blue number you wore at cousin Gloria's wedding will do nicely. You looked smashin' pet'" I said, but she promptly took a wobbler – went absolutely bananas. 'Can't be seen in that AGAIN' she screams. 'What will people think?'

'But that was 1972,' says I. 'Who the hell is gonna remember something you wore ONCE, a quarter of a century ago? The bride wasn't even born then! Abba were top of the pops! Heath was Prime Minister!'

'Ah well there y'are then,' she says with devastating female logic, 'how can I possibly wear anything that's 25 years old? Do you want me to be completely humiliated?'

"A little humiliation can sometimes be a lot cheaper," Netherwitton said thoughtfully. But it was no use – the man was beyond counselling.

Anyway, perhaps it was all this desperate chat about what to wear, that got me thinking about my own rather limited wardrobe – something I don't do very often. Well to be honest, I've never been what you might call "a snappy dresser'. Clothes are for warmth and modesty. Never been deeply into Armani suits and Calvin Klein shirts – more your "Scot's Gap designer peasant-wear" really.

In fact I've only ever had two suits in my entire sartorial life . . . and was reminded of the first one recently while burning some office rubbish. There was this pile of old invoices, statements and sundry correspondence, gathered up over the years and stuffed into cardboard boxes, their relevance long gone now. Time for a clean out.

Halfway through the incinerating exercise, a tiny slip of paper blew away in the breeze, and I chased after it down the field, just in case it might be something incriminating or embarrassing. It was both. It was the receipt for that early piece of worsted elegance, from "John Collier John Collier the window to watch". Remember them?

"Dark grey suit with waistcoat," it read. "Received with thanks the sum of twelve pounds." Twelve quid! Would you believe that?

Mind you, it was a RARE outfit. Lasted a couple of decades or more and often created quite a stir. Let me tell you, when that suit strolled nonchalantly into a room, the hum of conversation would stop abruptly, and people would take serious note. (I imagine it's the same when Imran Khan or Michael Caine walk into Stringfellows.) Though to be fair, with this J.C. suit, any hush might just possibly have been inspired by disbelief rather than breathless admiration.

Y'see the problem was, it simply didn't fit. Not my fault you understand – my shape isn't all THAT peculiar. Actually I don't believe the suit would've fitted any recognised form of animal life, ever! The jacket was ridiculous enough – wide body, short sleeves – but it was the trousers that really ruined the image.

Of course one wouldn't normally divulge such intimate details, but right from adolescence my inside leg measurement has been 33 inches. Now maybe when the Collier suit was purchased this information was unavailable, or even classified, who knows – but be that as it may, those trouser legs couldn't have been more than half that length at best. Consequently although they hung easily enough right from waist to winkle-pickers, there was this vast cavernous crotch area hovering just

48

above the knee. There were enormous unexplored regions of that suit I could never hope to occupy!

Nevertheless, it was worn with disarming modesty at weddings, funerals, and NFU dinner dances for several years – until at last I was persuaded to abandon it for a new model, purchased with a little more care this time from Marks 'n' Sparks.

The rest of the household were all for destroying the old one, but I would have none of it. Such a waste. So it was duly parcelled up and despatched to ease the plight of some unfortunate earthquake victims in southern Italy. No doubt it would be gratefully received. Indeed, I wouldn't be surprised if the local Mafia boss didn't get his eye on it straight away, and snap it up.

Well, y'never know – at this very moment some fashion-conscious Godfather could be sneaking away from the scene of yet another Sicilian slaughter wearing that same sophisticated John Collier ensemble. You can image the Carabinieri giving a statement to the press, can't you? "We have an excellent description of the villain," they'll say. "We're looking for a tall man with very short legs. We expect to make an arrest very soon . . ."

But enough of that suit – back to the father of the bride, poor chap. We left him as he scuttled away down the street to meet his wife and daughter – both no doubt already into rampant 'Imelda Marcos mode'. They still had to order the booze, the food, choose the hymns, meet the smiling vicar. More worry, more expense. Our friend was but a weary anxious figure when last we saw him, looking older and smaller by the minute. Like a lame spuggie surrounded by predatory pussy cats. He had no chance. Doomed.

I found myself smiling rather cruelly, until I remembered there was still an unwed daughter lingering seductively in the wings. Ye gods – should I make the lass an improved offer to elope? Perhaps impress upon her the lure of Las Vagas? She's quite a romantic girl – maybe a wedding at sea might appeal.

Well now, there's a thought. I used to know the skipper of the Kielder ferry quite well. If it came to the crunch, do you reckon he'd perform a special discount job? Well offshore on a moderate February afternoon might be a canny idea. Yes, I can see the lucky guests in yellow waterproofs and sou'westers – and not at all peckish – excellent! We could even invite Hello magazine.

Capital Punishment

THE first time I went to London (Smithfield Show, nineteen fifty something) four of us travelled down overnight in a noisy, smelly, Wolseley car. Another bloke and I shared the driving, while two young ladies sat in the back providing comfort and encouragement on the long, dangerous journey.

The heater didn't work, so whoever wasn't at the wheel cuddled up between the girls to keep warm. There were regular stops for flasked coffee and quick relieving forays over the hedge. (No motorway service stations then, y'know. No motorways!) It was like travelling overland to Afghanistan via Tow Law and Turkey, and by the time we reached the big city at dawn, old Wolseley had a leaky radiator and a slipping clutch, and the passengers were suffering from hypothermia.

We stayed at the Old Imperial Hotel in Russell Square, together with thousands of other Young Farmers from all over the country. It was a vast, crumbling, Victorian rabbit-warren of a building (since demolished and rebuilt, I think) – and at least half of those staying there never booked in or paid a bill. You just wandered the endless corridors until you found a pal or a party, and piled in. I remember nearly two dozen Northumbrians sharing one twin room for three nights, though maybe not all at the same time.

Downstairs the enormous two-acre lounge was always filled with various groups of card players, glee clubs and serious drinkers. On one occasion a group of lads from north of the Tyne were giving an enthusiastic rendering of "Cushy Butterfield", "Keep yor feet still Geordie hinny", and other patriotic anthems, when it became evident they were being overwhelmed by a Welsh choir belting out "Land of our Fathers". Well, you know what Welshmen are like when it comes to singing, and this lot were already full of London beer – it was way past their bedtime, and they wouldn't shut up. There they stood, five of them clinging together on top of a table, drowning out the northern chorus.

The Geordie boys stuck it for about quarter of an hour before they rose as one, lifted up the table with the Welshmen still in full flow, and carried the whole package out of the lounge (they were still singing) past the reception desk (still singing) and deposited them gently on an island in the middle of the street – still singing. There wasn't a lot of traffic about.

Getting to the capital is much easier now, especially when the train gets its act together, and rattles you to King's Cross in under three hours. Read a paper, cuppa tea, forty winks, and you're there – though even today I'm not entirely sure why anyone would want to go. Among the peasant population living soberly up the Wansbeck valley, any such excursion was always regarded as an unnecessary risk anyway. Even if the excuse was a visit to the big agricultural show at Earls Court, the older, wiser locals back home at the mart would shake their heads, give each other knowing looks and assume you were really up to no good. "Wat y' want t' gan there for?" they'd ask. "Muckle dorty noisy place!" And they were right of course, but it always seemed a bit of an adventure at the time . . . crossing the Tyne was like going abroad. You could see sights in Piccadilly that weren't all that common in Scot's Gap.

However, my impressions of any Smithfield trip were seldom agricultural. There's a limit to how many multi-coloured muck-spreaders and shampoo-ed Charolais bullocks I can look at. No, the pictures of London I come home with are always the same. At night a bunch of drop-outs, sleeping under a duvet of newspapers, in the doorway of Barclays' South Kensington branch. A few hundred yards up the street uniformed flunkies escorting rich, bejewelled guests from posh restaurants to personalised Rolls. All-day voices in the crowd babbling in a frenzy of foreign tongues (am I the only Englishman in town?). And pigeons everywhere, millions of them, many with toes missing, limping. Notices on station platforms urging travellers not to feed them because they're a health hazard. Why aren't the greedy little sods eating somebody's barley like proper pigeons, instead of begging for crumbs and having toes amputated on the District Line?

And the tube – that underground mechanical worm that carries commuters, shoppers and tourists every day from Turnham Green to Tottenham Court Road, from Mornington Crescent to Monument, cheek by jowl, rushing, pushing, clutching, hanging hot 'n' sticky, all with glazed acceptance on dull faces staring at the adverts.

The worst place I ever saw in London, the most terrifying experience, the most life-threatening episode of a long undistinguished career, was a whole hour spent trying to get out of Harrods. All I wanted was a toy tractor for a very small relation who lived in Chiswick. I was told the toy department at Harrods was the place. They have everything. Nobody told me everybody else on the planet would be there too . . . including the massed pipes and drums of the Argyll and Sutherland Highlanders (it's true!). They were marching straight towards me as I went in the door. A notice read "Toy Department fourth floor". I leapt on to an escalator and soared up up and away from Perfumes and Cosmetics, and the skirling pipes. But they followed me onto the moving staircase. Wherever I went, fighting for breath, for space, for toy tractors, tripping over small oriental people, bumping into big fat Americans, those kilted hordes would appear again bearing down on me, belting out some terrible Scottish dirge.

I grabbed a toy pistol (anything would do now) and fled through Lingerie and Soft Furnishings. The band was there as well. Down some stairs into Wines and Herbs, past Footwear and the Book Department, back among the bottles again. Panic – I was lost, going round in circles, pursued always by the pipes. I could die in here, never to be seen again. They'd probably sell me as a garden gnome (with out of season reduction). Then it dawned on me – there was only one way to escape. Ten minutes later I marched out into Knightsbridge at the rear of the Argyll and Sutherland Highlanders. It was a damn close-run thing, I tell you!

I know farmers are renowned as premier league complainers (the malady is inherited, I'm afraid there's no cure), but if pressed, most would be forced to admit how tremendously lucky they are to live "oot bye". The prospect of living and working in a big city would be enough t' mek y' eat yor bairns. Peasants seldom live next door to anybody – no embarrassing domestic noises on the other side of the wall, only a few sheep bleating miserably somewhere beyond the silage pit. The very idea of a street lamp or a bus stop at the bottom of the garden is simply too awful to contemplate. Ye gods, you might have a social worker as a neighbour, the bank manager living opposite, a VAT inspector in No. 23. There would be wives comparing tragedies over the fence, next door's cat abluting on your chrysanths. It hardly bears thinking about!

It certainly makes you realise how attractive dull detached isolation is. We're free to rant 'n' rave at our nearest and dearest in total privacy – free to kick the dog, mutilate an awkward yow – have a nervous breakdown all by ourselves. Nobody near, no twitching lace curtains, nobody borrowing the lawnmower or re-living his Sunday morning round of golf.

Furthermore, the average townie probably works for someone else (if he's working at all). What a terrifying thought! Even if he's quite important, on fifty thousand a year, indexed pension and company B.M.W., there'll almost certainly be another boss higher up, or a board of directors, watching his every move. There might be threats of redundancies, takeovers, lost orders, sexual harrassments. Far worse would be the constant pressure of being excessively nice to those above, and unreasonably reasonable to the prats below. Being your own gaffer is absolutely priceless, even if the bank is breathing down your neck. You're only responsible for your family and the Friesians. Get a lucky break and you might gain a bob or two. Make a cock-up and y' carry the can and serves y' right.

However, the most important pastoral privilege of all is there's simply no necessity to get tarted up every morning. There's nobody there to impress. The collie dog doesn't give a hoot what you look like. The sheep are only interested in a bale of hay. The family would be very suspicious indeed if they saw you going out in a clean shirt and a suit, smelling of aftershave – and rightly so.

Yes, there's a helluva lot to be said for a job where you don't have to dress up and commute with millions of others. Y' just climb out of bed, straight into a pair of wellies, and you're there!

Dogged By Amnesia

THE kids have long since flown the nest to seek their own overdrafts in the real world, and two black labradors have taken over the house. Thankfully these creatures seldom play heavy metal music while doing their homework, or giggle endlessly on the telephone. They don't wander about in suicidal depressions when their love life is in disarray, nor claim to be terminally ill with acne – but they do sit on my chair, and imagine they own the bloody place.

These canine lodgers live the life of Riley – in fact Mr Riley (whoever he was) would probably be insanely jealous of their lifestyle. Four-fifths of the known world don't live as well as these two wasters. They consume mountains of Robson and Cowan dog nuts, and indeed anything else left carelessly lying about. They've never been known to turn up their cold wet noses at anything – old boiled cabbage, bacon skins, lumpy congealed gravy, apple gowks, rotten tomatoes – everything goes, as if thrown into two bottomless dark incinerators.

They just eat and sleep – and smile a lot. They smile disarmingly after chewing the floor tiles in the kitchen. They smile self-consciously when caught peeing on the pansies. They smile apologetically after raiding the waste bin under the sink. They smile guiltily when asked where the rest of the fruit cake went. Visitors make a ridiculous fuss of them of course – they hold silly one-sided conversations with the dozy things, while the dogs wag and wobble and grin as if they understood every word. It wouldn't really matter if the people were blathering in Bulgarian or Swahili, and pinching the telly – provided there is a chance they might drop the merest morsel of food, a temporary slobbering adoration is assured.

My guest had managed to drink his coffee and protect a digestive biscuit just long enough to thwart the drooling dogs, and they'd gone back to doze in front of the fire, disappointed – one eye half open, just in case. "They have a canny life," he grinned. "I think I might come back as a labrador next time."

We'd been discussing (as people do) how quickly the years flew past now, faster than ever as we become older. They just seemed to nod and hurry away, as if bored by men who reminisce too much. The conversation was not in any way morbid you understand . . . in fact we were quite delighted to have got this far, having avoided the various perils of peasantry, such as cowping tractors, bad-tempered bulls, diseased sheep and excitable chain saws. But we both knew we had "peaked" some time ago.

It was the knees that went first, I think. Oh they're still there of course, just where you'd expect to find them, hidden away in their own dark knobbly little world, halfway down m' trouser legs – minding their own business most of the time – seldom exposed to public scrutiny or bright sunlight, except maybe occasionally on some secluded Mediterranean beach, where they quickly become embarrassed and turn bright red. For years they were nea bother, but now if I bend to pat those useless dogs, or talk to a small child, or pick a golf ball from the hole, they complain noisily like rusty bits of neglected farm machinery. I suppose that's exactly what they are really, and quite a few other parts have been showing distinct signs of wear and tear as well. I realise now (too late, of course) that none of them was ever properly maintained . . . often left outside on wet nights, abused at lambing time, never serviced on a regular basis.

Come to think of it, it was several springs ago when I first realised that even very old sheep, riddled with footrot, toe-nails like Chinese mandarins, coughing and wheezing as if on fifty Woodbines a day, could easily side-step past, leaving me pathetically clutching nowt but fresh air. It was long ago when policemen appeared to be no more than power-crazed teenagers prowling about in Pandas. When pretty women in short summer frocks stopped smiling back at the hairy auld twit who leered at them. When reps who came to buy, sell, or advise, were the same age as my own children, alleged experts with spots. When the children themselves abandoned any fragile pretence of parental respect, and replaced it with blank incredulity or amused resignation.

And yet, far more alarming than this inevitable march of time and the odd mechanical breakdown is the rapid deterioration of that stuff slopping about between m' lugs. You've guessed it – the mind is going too. In particular those little grey bits of semolina that control the memory. No, they were never brilliant either (at least I can remember that much). Hints for anniversaries and appointments always had to be left in strategic places – wee notes stuffed into m' wellies, on top of the kettle, in the biscuit tin, by the telephone. I once wandered round Newcastle for half a day wondering where I'd parked the car . . . eventually came upon it quite by accident, and still wasn't absolutely sure until I tried the key in the lock; couldn't remember the number.

On another occasion a daughter rang from a call-box and asked to be collected in Morpeth. "Right," I said, "set off and walk, I'll meet you in ten minutes." Then I put the phone down and promptly forgot about the poor lass. Luckily after a while she got a lift from somebody else, but she wasn't all that chuffed to find me having forty winks on the kitchen sofa.

That sort of thing is bad enough, but the really big problem is people's names. There's a vast black hole where Jacks and Jills, Janets and Johns all tumble through and disappear. The world is full of familiar faces without names. I'm constantly trapped in little groups who wait expectantly to be introduced by me. No chance – all they ever get is a vacant labrador-like grin as I desperately grope for clues in the mist. Does anyone else have this disorder, I wonder? What do they do? Create a diversion perhaps – pretend to have a quick cardiac arrest? Bluff their way out of it somehow – or hide in the loo till everyone's gone away?

A while ago I was playing golf with two fellas I hadn't met before, and was determined to get their names right. Make a serious effort, listen, remember. One was called Richard (I think) and the other was Brian – or was it Barry? No, it was definitely Brian, because I thought his voice sounded rather like Brian Redhead from Radio Four. O.K., concentrate –

Richard and Brian, Brian and Richard. I drummed the names into my skull for the first five holes, before feeling confident enough to use them out loud. "Good shot, Richard," I said generously, as he chipped onto the green. "Thank you,' he snarled without smiling, "but that's Richard over there in the rough . . . I'm Brian."

At one stage, desperately aware of this embarrassing block, I tended to stroll about head in the air, staring blankly at clouds and chimney pots, fairly confident there'd be very few folk up there I should recognise. "Arrogant sod,' they muttered, "passed by on the street yesterday, never said a word, didn't even see us . . . !"

Then for a time I went about smiling at everybody, just in case I was supposed to know them. However a lot of people concluded (reasonably enough) that anyone with a permanent silly grin on his face has to be a congenital idiot – perhaps even dangerous. You can't win.

One day in Morpeth I bumped into a bloke I knew well. I felt confident of that, but of course as soon as I met him, his name vanished completely. Not to worry, he would be a farmer, almost sure. He looked like a farmer, though admittedly it's harder to tell these days – some of them get all tarted up to go into town. And I think his hands were in his pockets.

"Hiya,"I said cheerily (a lot of people are called Hiya when you've got an affliction like mine), "so, how's life? You'll have had a bumper harvest likely, eh?"

"Harvest?" he said, obviously somewhat bewildered, "what harvest?"

Now at this point I should have simply hurled m'self under a passing bus, or leapt through Woolworth's window, – but like a fool, I persisted.

"Oh, don't you have any corn?" I asked. "All set-aside now, is it?"

"Look,"he said, "I don't know what you're on about. I work in the bank, have done for 20 years. I see you in there nearly every week!"

Well, I knew I'd met him somewhere. It's pathetic really.

When I got home the labradors barked as I opened the back door. For a brief moment they didn't seem too sure who I was – at least not until they'd had a real good sniff at my trouser leg – then they knew . . .

Well now, there's an interesting technique. I wonder if ? No, don't even think about it!

That's Show Business

THE setting is superb – a natural rural theatre built when Mother Nature was much younger. The stage set on a sheltered meadow down by the river, with a backcloth of well-dressed old trees rising up the banks beyond. A church steeple just visible, peeping through the branches. It's a village show like village shows used to be, were meant to be or at least as near as you'll find these days.

I suppose people once arrived by cart, on horseback, in traps pulled by cocky little ponies. They would be dressed up in best Sunday go-to-meetin' tweed suits, or long frocks and bonnets with ribbons attached. Now the car park is filled with Shoguns and Range Rovers, and although there are still a few hairy suits and Rogerson boots in evidence, today's gear is more likely to be jeans, T-shirt and trainers, or anorak and wellies.

The packaging might have changed a bit, but the weatherbeaten faces and the big hard hands are still there. This is definitely a country affair, run by farming folk. Not that "toonies" aren't welcome you understand, and there are two bonny country lasses on the gate to take their money.

Down in the field shorthorn cows are tied up under shady branches chewing the cud, while men in white coats pamper them, eyeing up the competition. Shepherds, with the worried look shepherds often wear, comb mule yowes, wipe the noses of blue-faced Leicesters. Swaledales and blackies talk among themselves. Collie dogs on baler twine leads wait their turn to show off.

Steady Clydesdales trot up and down in slow motion, looking just as their grandfathers did, in halters and hame sticks and bright brass medallions. Behind a blue Volvo, sitting on a beer crate, a lady is milking her goat. Over by the horse boxes pot-bellied ponies (not exceeding 14.2 hands) leap about like nervous ballerinas.

In the industrial tent there's a forest of dressed hazel sticks on display – pheasants and fishes carved on horn crooks. Needlework and scones, gingerbread and brandy butter, rhubarb jam and custard tarts, young Willy's best handwriting, fresh flowers arranged in a sugar bowl (Class 54).

On the public address system Maurice announces that a white van is parked in a silly place, and would the owner kindly move it as soon as possible, please.

The judges are at work now: experienced, respected men and women, recognised throughout the known world as leading authorities on yowes, sows, cows and cookery. They wear red badges and take their time . . . get it right . . . be fair: it's a big responsibility. Those two mule gimmers in pen number five might not be too disappointed if they only get a Highly Commended, but the shepherd certainly will be. Still, y'canna please everybody.

The show jumping has begun in the main ring. It's hardly Hickstead or Badminton, but it's nail-biting stuff all the same. A demented cob roars through the course destroying most of the obstacles. "Abigail Pettigrew on Desert Orchid, 24 faults," says Maurice sympathetically, "and will the owner of the white van move it at once, please . . . !"

Trade stands are touting for business. They'll sell you a blanket for your bed or your thoroughbred, a socket set for the handyman, heathers and hyacinths for the garden. Fresh cream and ice cream, hot dogs and cold beer.

Over by the trees young Mansells are racing oriental trikes around a track marked out by straw bales. Men dressed in old thermal underwear are wrestling, Cumberland-style, clasped together, turning lifting and twisting in a warlike waltz for the best of three falls. The loudspeaker hanging from a branch reports only six faults for Nicola Tomlinson on Shergar – and if the white van isn't shifted within the next five minutes, it'll be towed away by Charlie Forster's tractor!

The ladies' committee is serving lunch in the refreshment tent – ham, chicken and salad, brown buns and butter, fruit trifle and a pot of tea. I find myself sitting with the chairman and two of the sheep judges. Outside clouds are building up and "the forecast's not ower gud". Will the rain hold off till it's all over?

"Well, at least you'll not have much harvest to worry about in these parts." said I.

"What? Y'canna grow corn up here," the Swaledale judge snorted dismissively. "Nowt but bloody yowes and a few lean suckler cows. It's a hard life, not like the land o' Goshen where ye come from, y'knaa – ye lot wi' your fower tons o'wheat t' the acre . . . y' divvent knaa you're born. We have winter for eight months!" He made it sound as if we were in Outer Mongolia.

The other judge nodded his agreement. "They wouldn't know what work was doon bye." he said. "Just sit on their arse in an air-conditioned tractor cab aal day!"

I felt I could hardly let it pass at that. "They have lambin's in the Wansbeck valley as well,' I protested, "and they lose money every year feedin' your little expensive calves . . . and it can snow there as well, you know."

"Y' don't know what real snow is, man,' grunted the Swaledale man. "Colossal drifts, we're blocked in every year . . . !"

When the trifle came I asked if any of them had managed to fight their way out of this desolate poverty-stricken hinterland for a wee holiday. "Oh, aye, the missus and me had a few days away after the first silage cut." said the other judge. "Just a few days, mind y'."

"Where did y' get to?" I asked.

"Barbados." he said, without looking up from his pudding. "It was very canny."

Back in the arena, a man with six collie dogs was shepherding a posse of ducks through an obstacle course and into a horsebox. It was quite impressive, but perhaps the ducks had done it before. The brass band was belting out its repertoire of breezy village show tunes. All the judging was completed now. Clear rounds in the show jumping were racing against the clock. The wrestling was into the final stages as well, four young lads built like byres ready for the final struggle. Glory and a few quid in prize money beckoned.

Maurice announced the winners of the children's fancy dress (everybody got a rosette) and pleaded for the owner of the white van to report to the secretary's tent immediately. The threat of Charlie Forster's tractor hadn't worked, not least because Charlie had already gone home in it. Maybe the committee would now assemble and throw the van into the river.

In the secretary's tent the trophies stood gleaming on a trestle table – a fortune in polished silver – about 30 assorted cups, rose bowls and tankards, collected over 150 years. They were for the handsomest shorthorn, the fleetest pony, the bonniest ewe lamb, the choicest cherry cake, the best border bitch. It was time to give them away.

Four men picked up the table and, without losing even a trophy lid, carried the whole lot out into the main ring, where a posse of stewards checked the list of winners, and gathered the successful men and beasts into ordered groups. Placid cattle waited on white rope halters, dogs sat quietly by their masters, horses pranced impatiently on tight reins, shepherds leaned on fancy sticks. The crowd watched and waited on the grassy bank, some looking skywards as a few drops of rain fell. Maurice was eager to get on with it.

"Ladies and gentlemen, the Arthur Thompson Perpetual Challenge Cup for novice jumping goes to (theatrical pause) . . . Jemima Johnson-Smythe on Priestpopple Popsy the Third!" This was Olympic gold. The crowd applauded, the band played, mother glowed, and Priestpopple Popsy the Third was urged nervously towards the Perpetual Challenge Cup. The beaming Jemima stretched down over the pony's neck to accept her prize. It wasn't easy. Popsy was performing a sort of equine tango, but Jemima managed to grab the cup and smile an anxious thank you before the petrified Popsy spun round and away.

"Next, the William Weatherspoon Rose Bowl for best heavy horse, mare or gelding three years old and upwards is awarded to . . ." That's as far as Maurice got.

Behind him Jemima, still struggling to control her excited gee-gee and cling on to her prize, had dropped the cup. It clattered to earth and the lid flew off into the line of other ponies waiting for their moment of triumph. Desert Orchid galloped backwards, leaving a startled Abigail dismounting between his lugs. This encouraged another frantic filly to panic in ever-decreasing circles towards the rows of cattle and sheep.

Two big, dozy shorthorns awoke to see several mad horses bearing down on them, and decided to leave immediately. Their handlers, suddenly airborne on the end of white halter ropes, had no chance – they were obliged to go too. Whitfield Empress Wilhelmina, heavy with calf, faced with a trestle table loaded with bright shiny things and several well-dressed official looking gentlemen, was in no mood to be delayed. She probably wasn't sure where she was going, but had already decided elsewhere was a better place to be, and nowt was going to stop 'er.

Stewards waved their sticks, Maurice waved his microphone, the chairman waved his prize list, but the cow jumped straight over the table, scattering engraved trophies and bewildered stewards in all directions. For several minutes it looked as if a sudden hurricane had swept through the showground. Desperate shepherds clung to terrified prizewinning tups, agitated dogs barked, canny auld Clydesdales kicked at anything within range, and wild-eyed ponies careered about the field with squealing nubile maidens hanging around their necks. Wilhelmina was heading towards the car park with her man still attached, his white coat covered in clarts.

But this show had been going for 153 years – one disappearing cow and a few petrified ponies couldn't disrupt tradition now. Already the scattered trophies were being collected, the trestle table re-erected, upturned stewards dragged back on to their feet and dusted off. Maurice was back on the mike. "The J.W. Sanderson Rose Bowl for best working collie is won by . . . The Journal Silver Salver for champion Suffolk goes to . . . Winner of The Tynedale Cup is . . ."

There was admittedly just a little confusion as some folk went off with the wrong trophy – or got the right trophy with the wrong lid – but that was only to be expected. The brave stewards sorted it all out in the end, and the rain didn't come before everyone had their prize.

Wilhelmina had reached the road before she ran out of steam, and now stood heaving and slavering on the grass verge. Her minder didn't look too frisky either, but he'd hung on like a good 'un.

A line of vehicles was piling up in the car park, full of people eager to be off home. They wouldn't get far – not until the owner of the white van blocking the exit was persuaded out of the beer tent.

Arrivederci Shilbottle

TALK to any farmer these days and he'll tell you he's pretty fed up.

"Oh really," I hear you snigger. "So what's fresh? Farmers always grumble, don't they?" If it's not the weather, it's the government, the collie dog, the lambing or the long-suffering wife. Maybe even the whole lot at once. There's either a drought or there's too much rain. The missus wants ANOTHER frock (her second since the coronation)! Moss is in pup to that doberman cross-dachshund from the vicarage. The sheep are wandering about in the barley field and the government is wandering about in disarray. Farmers have a well-earned reputation as premier league complainers. It's in the very nature of the job – not least because Mother Nature can always foil the best laid plans of the most imperturbable peasant.

But now there's something else to grouse about, something even more soul-destroying and sinister than set-aside, salmonella, or beef on the bone.

Recently a new all-consuming pest has descended on the countryside. A locust-like plague of paper is blowing over from the continent, and threatens to suffocate life as we once knew it. There are now so many forms, maps and questionnaires to fill in that some farmers are spending all their working day stuck in an office. Those ruddy weatherbeaten complexions grow pale, wellies stand forlorn and abandoned at the back door, hard gnarled hands (once the size of shovels) shrivel to slender effeminate things with clean fingernails.

His wife is sick o' the sight of 'im, constantly getting in the way of her vacuum cleaner. He's on the phone, drinking tea, nervously chewing a biro, sobbing pitifully into his pocket calculator, as he tries to comprehend the mountain of ambivalent gobbledegook churned out by the MAFFia. Gone are the old familiar pictures of normal, lovable country folk toiling in the field, the man ploughing his lonely furrow, or leaning thoughtfully on a horned stick surveying his husbandry – or perhaps advising the wayward rambler where to go next. He hasn't time for all that rural nonsense, not now! There's a whole lot of clerkin' to be done, deadlines to meet, quota applications to fill in, a host of new rules and regulations waiting to confound the poor bloke every day of the week. From Durham to Dorset the land echoes to the cries of bewildered peasants.

So what's going on? Well, it's this crazy European thingie, isn't it? The sprouting Brussels bureaucracy is already out of control. It's as if you got up'one fine morning and found your tidy garden full of nettles. Everything you'd carefully nurtured suddenly overwhelmed – petunias smothered, lobelia strangled, marigolds choked – and the spuggies twittering with a French accent!

From all this you might reasonably conclude that I'm what's known as a Euro-sceptic. Wrong! I'm absolutely positively agin it!

In fact I believe anyone in favour probably requires serious counselling. It's a daft idea. An endless gravy train fuelled by fraud, chicanery, greed, duplicity and nonsense. Another vast government machine (on top of our own Westminster lot), spending zillions of Euros to justify their very existence. Sitting jabbering in new ivory towers, dreaming up yet more silly legislation. Concocting an inedible stew of spaghetti, sauerkraut, paella, feta cheese, and heaven knows what other ethnic delicacies that everyone is obliged to swallow. It will surely give us bellyache.

Of course, I realise these opinions are born of a parochial childhood spent mostly in the company of sheep, and an inbred conviction that Alnwick was probably the birthplace of civilisation. But to put a Rothbury peasant under the same flag as a Bavarian in silly leather shorts is just asking for trouble!

I remember once being persuaded on a package holiday to Corfu and watching a Corfiot farmer gather HIS harvest. It was definitely a much simpler task than combining soggy barley on a dull day at home in Northumberland. This fellow earned his living from a few olive trees planted long ago by Romans, and when the fruit ripened he simply placed a net under each tree and waited for a windy night. If perchance the wind didn't blow, not t'worry – he just mounted his battered old tractor and drove it repeatedly at the tree until all the reluctant olives fell to earth. Next came the question of transport – how would he collect and deliver this bountiful harvest?

At this stage Costas (all Greeks are called Costas) obviously considered his job was finished, and quietly retired to the local taverna. It was Mrs Costas who now appeared and gathering up the four corners of each net, heaved them onto a donkey, and led the poor animal off to the nearby olive press. Nea bother, end of harvest – another ouzo and a packet of garlic crisps if you please, barman.

It was the cushiest farming system I've ever seen, and it doesn't take a visionary to realise THAT lifestyle has little in common with a potato grower in Lincolnshire, a bacon producer in Devon, or even a farmer's wife in Northumberland. However, Costas is now filling in the same forms, and probably claiming a subsidy on more olive trees than all the Romans ever planted anywhere.

The very first time I bravely ventured on to the continent was years ago as a naive spotty youth. Another spotty youth and I travelled by train to Italy. I imagine the plan was to drink a little wine, lie in the warm Mediterranean sun, and astonish any available signorinas with our sophisticated North Country charm. Anyway the sun shone, the wine flowed and it was a canny holiday. The problems came on the return journey.

We had to change trains at Milan, and after dumping our bags on the Paris-bound express, we sauntered off in search of a final bottle of Chianti to ease the long trip north. Good idea, eh? Unfortunately, we climbed back on to the wrong train while the right one pulled out of the station, taking with it all the luggage, including my passport. Ah well, eccentric Englishmen have been wandering aimlessly about Europe for centuries. Foreigners just shake their heads and shrug their shoulders. They understand.

So we eventually boarded another train and began the journey again, a full day behind our baggage. At the Italian-Swiss frontier there were two passport checks. On the Italian side I flashed an out-of-date driving licence at the official, and he seemed quite impressed with that. However, the Swiss lads were not entirely satisfied. They hauled me from the train and threw me into prison, apparently convinced they'd caught a major international spy – maybe even The Jackal. It looked rather dodgy for a while: visions of incarceration for years. I couldn't see any diplomatic deals being made for the likes of me. I sent a desperate message home. "Detained at Swiss border," it said. "Help!"

Next morning came the interrogation by a policeman, armed to the teeth and not at all sympathetic.

"Name?" he barked. At least that's what I thought he said, so I told him.

The next question sounded like "Where you come from?" Now at this point I should have said "England", but for some inexplicable reason I was much more specific. "Shilbottle", I said with a winning smile. This completely bamboozled the man. He felt obliged to summon his superiors, who went into a huddle and babbled away in a state of some confusion. It seemed they hadn't heard of Shilbottle. I got the impression they might even suspect it to be a notifiable disease. Or then again, maybe the man had asked a different question altogether – how would I know? Be that as it may, I believe Shilbottle proved to be an inspired answer, and by teatime I was released. I think they were quite relieved to be rid of this idiot.

Of course, such adventures won't be possible in the new "improved" Europe. There will be no frontiers, no passports. Spotty youths, fraudsters and drug-peddling godfathers will just stroll through the old borders with no more inconvenience than stepping over a puddle.

On that occasion the passport and our bags were waiting in Paris, and three days late we chugged into Newcastle Central station at midnight. I got a lift up the A1, and walked the last few miles to the farm. I half expected father to be waiting anxiously for the return of his prodigal son, perhaps even in conference with the Foreign Office, but he was out playing cards somewhere, and the door was locked. I was obliged to climb up a drainpipe, scramble through the skylight on the back kitchen roof, and tumble down onto a pile or dorty weshin'. It was good to be back in the "real world" again. It always is.

Odds Against

I ONCE knew a bloke who would happily wager on two flies crawling up a window pane, or even two raindrops trickling down. That's if he could find anyone daft enough to take the bet.

He gambled on horses, football, dogs and pigeons. Played three-card brag twice a week and dominoes (a shilling a game) every night in the pub. He was not a millionaire.

Me? I was never a gambler. To be honest, never had the bottle for it. Hate losing. The occasional modest flutter on the National or the Derby perhaps, or the leek club raffle — but nothing serious and seldom successful.

Maybe farming was always a big enough lottery. The job depends so much on the fickle finger of Michael Fish. His splodges and isobars can make or break the best laid plans. Mother Nature can be a bosom pal and a heartless adversary, both on the same day.

You can do everything right, play a blinder . . . then El Niño nips in and scores the winner in extra time. "Offside!" you cry, but to no avail. The game is lost, and you stagger off to bury the dead sheep, or sow the crop all over again.

I was further discouraged by a couple of wayward pals (lovely lads) who continually put their pocket money on a succession of unco-operative gee-gees. These boys were experts: very keen, lived in the fast lane, and were extremely knowledgeable on all aspects of horseflesh. Or at least to hear them chattering away you might suppose so.

But of course (as with most gamblers) one only hears of the winning wager. Gamblers tend to be like that. They appear to have a rather comforting malady called 'selective amnesia'. The four-legged friend can fall at the first fence, but blinkered optimism continually leaps over all disappointments. The 3.30 at Chepstow will put everything right. And indeed it might . . . for a while.

This stout-hearted attitude was vividly demonstrated on my one-and-only visit to 'The Dogs'. "Essential viewing," says my dedicated gambling mate. "Broaden your education. Part of life's rich pageant," he says. "You'll have an entertaining evening." And I certainly did.

To a naïve country boy, anxiously clutching his loose change, it all looked very classy and professional. There were restaurants, bars, bookies, pretty girls, the Tote, and a miscellany of seasoned betting folk with Bogart raincoats and Steve McQueen eyes. And of course those lean, sleek hounds eager to charge from their traps and pursue a mechanical rabbit.

Well, you can't just turn up at a do like this for a pie and a pint. A small careful investment is called for. But which animal to entrust with my ten bob? I hadn't a clue.

Enter Alfie. He was appointed as my 'minder' to see me alright on the night. I'd never met this greyhound guru before, and he didn't look particularly successful. No fat cigar, camel hair coat, Gucci shoes. In fact he looked a bit like I imagine a child molester looks — bleary eyes, unshaven, scruffy mac, tab dangling from the corner of his mouth, not many teeth. A bit creepy, really — but apparently he knew all about the dogs.

"I'll mark yer card for y'," he whispers, like someone about to reveal classified parish shenanigans. In fact not only did he know the dogs, he knew what they'd had for lunch, their recent form, the handler, the trainer, the vet and the owner's missus. He watched the animals parade, and noted if they paused for a pee or broke wind. Nothing, it seemed, was left to chance.

"First race, put yer money on Blaydon Bandit; canna be beat," he advises. And sure enough, the creature won by several lengths.

"Second race, Whickham Wanderer should do the business." And he did.

"Third? Not sure about this one," he mutters apologetically. "Maybe split yer bet between Fenham Fury and Consett Cavalier . . . should be okay."

They came in first and second! And so it went on. The man was a genius. Surely he didn't need to work? He must already have a stately home somewhere in the Tyne Valley, a luscious blonde mistress cunningly concealed in Cramlington. A Jag in the car park, probably.

There were six races that night, and Alfie picked the winner every time. I followed his advice for the first three, then quit like the devout coward I am — bought the man a few beers, and estimated I was a tenner richer after all expenses. Champion. That would do me nicely. But Alfie wasn't finished yet.

The management put on an extra race, and our hero duly wagered all his considerable winnings (and I mean a few hundred quid) on this final flutter of the evening. I suppose he had every reason to anticipate a real killing. Another carefully considered 'sure thing'. He couldn't lose, could he?

Of course, his 'sure thing' came a disappointing fourth, and Alfie was back to square one again. I gave him a lift home and paid for his fish'n'chips supper. He said he'd had a 'tremendous night'!

Other than a few point-to-points in a reckless (huntin') youth, my sole real racing experience was at Gosforth Park. They hold a meeting on the Friday eve before the Northumberland Plate. Maybe you're a regular. If so, you'll know it's in June, and especially if the weather is kind, it can be a very pleasant social occasion. If you come away into pocket, that's a bonus.

I need only tell you of the first event on the card.

Never having been to such a proper horsey gathering before, I determined to do some serious research. At least give m'self a chance . . . dilute some of the mystery. I bought the Racing Post, the Express, the local Journal, consulted form guides, the opinions of Hotspur and Gypsy Rose Lee — the lot. My knowledge was (albeit briefly) almost encyclopaedic.

Anyway, the first race looked like a walk-over for Golden Miracle (or whatever his name was). He was odds on. Those in the know all agreed — the other horses were just there to make up the numbers. Every tipster in the land had him picked. He hadn't come all the way from Newmarket to finish second. He'd probably win the Derby some day, they said. He was that good. Half an hour before the 'off' you couldn't even get a bet on. The bookies were all convinced as well . . . no contest.

The lady who accompanied me on this equine adventure put her five penn'orth on a grey thing. Not because she had inside information, not because its mother was well bred, not because Lester Piggott was driving it — but because it was grey . . . and pretty. And yes, you've guessed it. Golden Miracle is still out there in the woods somewhere for all I know, and the grey thing romped home with a smile on its pretty face, at about 20-1.

I haven't been back since, convinced I was simply out of my depth in such devilishly sophisticated company. It's a world that revolves around a temperamental and unpredictable animal (often with a small bandy-legged rascal on its back) where hordes of 'blinkered' punters peer into big black binoculars (as if it were a crystal ball) and force money into the outstretched hand of a loud man with a blackboard and a bit of chalk. A man who will almost certainly drive merrily home in a Mercedes. It's all too risky for me.

But then let's face it — I'm a wimp really. Not smart enough or bold enough to play the happy-go-lucky gambler. The bug that apparently bites the likes of Alfie finds nothing tasty here, even if he sucks really hard. It's a hopeless case.

Even away from the track, in the normal world, I can too easily pick the lame horse. This is the shrewd old gadgie who cleverly with-draws his modest savings from the Netherwitton Building Society, only to watch it transform itself into a bank two days later, and reward loyal investors with free shares and a big fat bonus!

This is the entrepreneurial peasant most likely to invest in a thousand Rhode Island reds, just as some earnest politician declares all eggs to be terminal. The man who mows his hay the day a sudden deep depression settles over the Wansbeck, and several weeks later is obliged to bale black inedible muck as his farming neighbours try hard not to giggle. The intrepid traveller on the flight to 'paradise' (knees up about his lugs) who is overwhelmed by overlapping overweight alcoholics determined to be legless on arrival. And there's a five-hour delay, of course.

No, we can't all hit the jackpot, and many of us are naturally quite reluctant to put the pension on some fickle creature we've never even met.

In fact, this piece was originally intended to link up with a visit to Kelso races, where *The Northumbrian's* very own thoroughbred animal was entered. Sadly however, a few days before the meeting, the noble beast turned up for training with a sick note from his mother asking to be excused strenuous exercise. He had a sore throat or a groin strain or something . . . and in the end neither of us got there. It probably saved me a few quid.

Which reminds me of a neat wee quote heard recently from a not-very-successful professional sportsman. Interviewed after yet another unrewarding performance, he smiled ruefully and said: "Ah well, look at it this way — I started out with nothing . . . and I've still got most of it left!"

Command Performance

IT was way back in the twenties when the parish council decided they needed a village hall – somewhere to hold whist drives, leek shows, WI meetings and the like. Nowt flashy y' understand, as long as the building was weatherproof, had electric light and piped water, a flush toilet and floorboards with enough bounce to cope with the occasional eightsome reel; that would do nicely.

Of course, it would be almost impossible to build the thing today. Bureaucracy would go berserk. The Department of the Environment would have to be involved. The Health and Safety Executive, the Council for the Protection of Rural England, the county council, the borough council, would all consult endlessly. The EEC might even send a fact-finding mission over from Brussels. The chief planning officer would probably insist on a concrete and glass edifice, big enough to accommodate Northumbria Water seminars. Eventually, after a decade of debate, it would be decided the plans for this "cultural community centre" were (after all) quite unrealistic – and they'd spend the money on a five-star rehabilitation hostel for young underprivileged urban burglars instead.

Yesterday it was much simpler. A delegation from the village trundled up to the "big hoose", cap in one hand, forelock in the other, and humbly put their proposal to the squire. "Splendid idea," says the squire, "you can have that piece of waste ground beside the post office – and what's more, I'll even lend you some money to build it!"

And he did – interest free. From estimates to completion took less than a year, and the total bill was seven hundred and sixty nine pounds, fourteen shillings and tuppence! Alright, it rattles a bit in stormy weather but it's still there – and tonight people are queuing to get in.

Tonight is Northumbrian Night, and the evening air is filled with the chatter and blather of local folk as they fill up the seats.

"Room for a little 'n here . . ."

"Bunk alang a bit, Annie . . ."

There's a bar in the cloakroom, and everybody wants a drink to take into the show. "Three pints o' scotch and a packet o' vinegar crisps when y've got a minute, pet . . ."

An anxious line is forming at the gents already. The ladies seem better controlled or better prepared, but a few desperate lads have gone into the field, behind the hedge.

"Been t' the mart the day, Charlie?"

"Aye, canny trade man . . ." He looks skywards where only a handful of stars are scattered about the heavens.

"It's ganna rain," he says, and as if to confirm this beyond all reasonable doubt: "moderate forecast."

By 7.30 it's a full house, and the master of ceremonies is eager to get things going. He checks with the little group of artists huddled together in the passage. (No fancy dressing rooms here – no star on any door.) Some of them feel in need of a small whisky, just to steady the nerves.

"Who's on first?"

"It'll be Burb (Bob) likely – aalwuziz."

"Where's the fiddler? Is he not here yet?"

A performer from Pegswood strums a few practice bars on his guitar, clears his throat, lights another cigarette. The comedian checks his notes, wonders whether to use the story about the vicar and the barmaid (it went down well enough at Mitford, but y' never can tell). He takes a sneaky look at the audience. They seem to be enjoying themselves, and the "proceedin's" haven't even started yet. Of course there's nothing overly sophisticated or trendy about this lot – well, I mean it's hardly a Harold Pinter first night, is it? You'll not find many bow ties, long frocks and tiaras in a place like this. This is not the sort of crowd who are seen regularly at the opera. They're not likely to get over-excited by some world-famous contralto (the size of a canny Charolais) dressed in cardboard armour over a purple nightie, howling away in German while a chorus of desolate hessian-clad slaves wail in sympathy, her baritone lover in thermal underwear and a short waistcoat prancing about waving his spear and the orchestra plays something from a different (even more turgid) affair altogether.

No, the Northumbrian Night is not on that level – nowhere near so highbrow and "cultural". It's not subsidised by the Arts Council either, probably because all the performers are more or less normal. And let's face it, nobody in this neck o' the woods would turn up to hear a hairy unemployed weirdo chanting Nicaraguan folk-poems. Any precious thespian silly enough to don make-up and tights and give us a few lines from King Lear would probably be heard in polite silence – then hoyed oot! This audience wants music to make their feet move, jokes about a life they recognise, songs with a melody they remember, and might whistle on the way home.

Quarter of an hour behind schedule the show begins. The MC mounts the stage, and modestly informs the assembled throng how lucky they are to be here. "The artists we have tonight are world-class," he says, "and y' get your supper as well – tremendous value!" You also get his jokes, which range over a wide area of human behaviour and experience, often involving some unsuspecting victim in the hall. This man knows everybody on the planet.

Robert and his three-piece band get the entertainment going – reels and jigs and marches played with such smiling effortless skill, you might briefly be persuaded that any fool could do it. They never pause, one tune is spliced into another, toes tap, hands clap, fingers on the table pretend to play along. Then rapturous applause, more beer, more jokes from the chairman, and the lad from Pegswood comes on.

He tells us how incompetent he is, says he's not sure what to do really, apologises for beginning with a totally unsuitable song about two fellas sleeping in the same bed (shock-horror!) and promptly launches into "Keep your feet still Geordie hinny" – with the audience roaring the chorus. He follows with a gentle flute solo, and then picks up the banjo to belt out that famous ballad aboot the worm. "Wheest lads had yer gobs, ah'll tell yuz aal an aaful story . . ." The man could perform nicely at the Palladium or Las Vegas – except they might not fully understand every word he said.

The fiddler has arrived. Now to my unmusical ear there are two undeniable things to say about violin music. A violin played badly is probably the most appalling noise on earth, on a par with whingein' bairns and Michael Jackson. However, in the hands of a master it can be one of the most beautiful sounds imaginable. This man is a master. There's not a whisper or a cough from the audience as he plays a soft, slow, lyrical piece, composed by some love-lorn highlander – but they gallop along with him when he lets rip with a selection of high-speed polkas. Brilliant stuff.

74

The MC is up on the stage again to announce the next act, and tell more jokes. Where does he get them? Not from a Christmas cracker, that's for sure. Anything remotely risque is greeted with hoots of laughter and shrieks of astonishment from a covey of old dears – as if they'd never heard such outrageous things before in their sheltered rural lives.

Next comes an accordion player, who quietly settles on a chair, straps himself onto his machine, and smiling straight ahead, allows his fingers to dance over the keys apparently with a mind of their own. It's country dance music, it's happy music, and we yell for more.

The highlight of the comedian's turn is an unlikely telephone conversation between the secretary of the leek club and the Queen, wondering if she'd be good enough to present the prizes next Saturday night. "Aye, w'knaa it's short notice, hinny, but Kevin Keegan let w' doon y' see – the lads are playin' at Tot'num that day . . . Oh sartinly y'll git yer suppa, an' wor lass'll mek up the spare bed . . . What's that? . . . Oh aye, yor Charlie can cum an' aal – he'll m'be want t' hev a chat wi' the leeks anyways!"

An old hill shepherd scrambles up on to the boards. It's not easy – well, his knees aren't what they used t' be – not after a lifetime battling with blackie yowes. He seems in no hurry though: moves a chair, gets himself comfortable, brings the microphone down to his level, and scraffles about in his coat pocket. Whatever he's looking for doesn't seem to be there. He scraffles about in his trouser pocket . . . where is it? What's he doing? The audience think it's part of the act. Eventually from somewhere inside his waistcoat he produces the mouthorgan. But he isn't ready yet – it's filled up with crumbs and fluff since the last performance, and it has to be cleaned out. He taps it on his knee, inspects the debris, brushes it away. He appears to contemplate the beams in the roof for a while, then (just as it was becoming a mite embarrassing for everybody except him) he cups the instrument in his big hands, slowly raises it to his weatherbeaten face, and blows. He sucks and blows for quarter of an hour after which, perhaps at a more urbane gathering, he might have received a standing ovation. Not here though; they never go that far. Nobody would expect such exotic displays of appreciation. Nevertheless, they're still applauding long after he's clambered down from the stage. And he never said a word.

There's a bonnie lass who sings . . . soars like a bird to the highest notes – nea bother. Another dubious joke from the MC, and to round off the evening all the musicians gather in a kind of country jam session. No sheet music, no discussions, no self-indulgent pronouncements – they just play. Robert starts up his accordion and the rest follow. It looks so easy – but then it always does when you're watching people who know what they're doing.

So that's it. The bar did a roaring trade and the takings are spirited away for the night. The raffle is drawn, the dirty dishes washed up, the village hall fund solvent for another year. Performers and audience head for home in the rain. It's gone midnight.

"Canny night eh, Charlie?"

"Tremendous, man. Beats the bloody telly anytime!"

Field Of Experience

STARING south out of the window, over the untidy garden, past the smelly sheep pens, across the Scot's Gap road, you can see the same fields that have lain there for maybe 200 years, divided like a quilt by wandering hedgerows and dark, quiet woods. The view stretches away as far as Shaftoe Crags, where (it seems from here at least) you might easily drop off the edge of the world into oblivion – or even County Durham. The picture hasn't changed much since we flitted here from the coast, way back when the royals were still mysterious superstars, and Hartburn had a village school.

Well, it has changed actually, if you know where to look. The fields are more or less the same shape and size (there's no prairie here), but for a start the gates are a lot wider these days. Monster tractors, and combines as big as a Gosforth semi, now squeeze through to plough, cultivate, or harvest a sea of cereals. On the little bit of pasture still remaining sheep graze cheek by jowl according to the ewe quota, and some bullocks away in the middle distance chew the cud, oblivious of their new European birth certificates. Here and there, scattered about the landscape, the odd desolate field lies unhusbanded, apparently unloved, abandoned to the set-aside culture of the day.

Once upon a time I was the bloke responsible for at least some of this window landscape – the fella who decided what grew where, and buried those sheep who didn't wish to be part of his master plan. None of this is in my custody now: better by far just to look at the scenery and remember less complicated farming days.

Take that field over there for instance – the one with the ditch running through the middle. It's called Tile Sheds, because long ago men dug clay there to make drainpipes and roof tiles. I once went berserk in that field. It was early one morning in lambing time, when I found most of the sheep in a heap about three deep up against the fence. The reason was obvious: halfway along the ditch a massive Alsatian dog the size of a horse was threatening to devour one poor auld yow (nearly all my sheep were poor auld yowes). She'd been hounded into the water, and now couldn't get out because her fleece was soaked, sodden and heavy. The terrified thing was on the brink of cardiac arrest as the dog prepared to make his final assault.

If I'd had the 12-bore I would certainly have shot the villain, but the only weapon I carried was a stick. Furthermore, my constant companion, Sweep the wonder collie, had suddenly remembered a previous appointment elsewhere. Not that he would have stood much chance against this killer – he'd worked that out pretty quickly, and indeed if I'd paused to consider the seriousness of the situation, I might have withdrawn as well.

But I didn't think. The very idea of some murderous beast making the lambing even more soul-destroying than usual filled me with outrage and a totally uncharacteristic bravado. Like some demented red Indian, half-crazed on fire water, I charged the "wolf", wielding the stick and screaming obscenities. I didn't even consider that he might prefer me to a bit of old mutton, or what breathless state I might be in by the time I reached him a hundred yards away. But as you may know, hell hath no fury like a shepherd in a bad fettle, and luckily the creature took one astonished look at the approaching nutcase – and fled. I carried the gun for a week after that, but he was no more bother. I would probably have missed 'im anyway.

Over to the right, that's the Cottage Field. I remember we almost had a serious fire in there. It must've been in August I suppose – harvest time. We'd cut the barley, and a neighbouring farmer was baling the straw. Picture the scene: lovely day, strong west wind, everything bone dry – perfect. This fella on his tractor pulling a red McCormack baling machine and, behind that, a "sledge" collecting the bales into rows to stack up later. (Almost everybody produces big round bales now, but in those days we only made little oblong ones.)

As you know, bales are tied with twine, and the twine came in paper bags. The tractor driver decided to burn these empty paper bags, rather than allow them to blow away and clutter up the countryside. Huge mistake! On his next journey round the field his sledge picked up the dying embers, and as he proceeded merrily on his way, no doubt whistling a happy tune in his cab, the bales in the sledge began to burn. Within a few minutes the man was trailing a mobile fire. It's not often you see a bright red tractor pulling a bright red baler followed by a raging inferno! Eventually (maybe he sniffed disaster in the breeze) he looked round to see what was happening, and panicked. He tripped the gate at the rear of the sledge and deposited his blazing load in the middle of some other bales. These promptly caught fire as well, and the flames went quickly on the west wind across the stubble right to the hedge. That caught fire too, and for a while we had visions of a biblical calamity reaching to the North Sea. Luckily the postman, the milkman and a few other passers-by prevented the flames from leaping over the road, and half an hour later the fire brigade had everything more or less under control. All except a rather shaky tractor driver.

To be fair, you can't actually see the River Field from this window. However, as we're rambling on about adventures in fields, we'll include this one. It's a big field, over 30 acres, and it runs all the way down to the Hart. There you'll find a ford carrying an old cart track over the river and away to the north. A few years ago there was a man living on the far side who drove his little Morris Minor over this ford every morning on his way to work. He seemed to manage the outward journey well enough, but at night he often stopped for a few jars with the lads, and sometimes this made it difficult for him to negotiate the route home. It was a rough, narrow, clarty track at the best of times, and on really serious alcoholic evenings you could bet your life he'd go off the road – maybe even slide into the river – and then stagger up to the farm and ask me to drag him out with a tractor.

One night in darkest February I was about to have m' supper. It had been pouring for days and now, long after dark, it was still chuckin' it doon. It was good to be inside, work finished for the day, wellies off, fire lit – champion. Then the phone rang. It was our friend from over the river.

"For God's sake come quickly," he pleaded. "The car's stuck in the middle of the ford!"

"Alright," says I wearily. "I'll come down as soon as I've had something t'eat . . . 20 minutes."

"No, NOW!" he cried desperately. "Come now. The river's flowing at a helluva rate and the car is being pushed off the edge of the ford. It'll be swept away before long!"

I was trying to sound calm. "Don't worry," I said. "We'll drag the thing out before it gets very far . . ."

"But you don't understand," he spluttered. "M' mother-in-law's still sittin' on the back seat!"

When I got there the old lady was staring blankly into the night, as the Morris crept inch by inch towards the deep pool below the crossing. The water was up to her knees. I offered to give her a piggy-back to dry land but she wouldn't move . . . wouldn't speak. We opened both car doors and allowed the river to run straight through. That seemed to take some of the pressure off, at least the car stopped moving sideways and eventually we got a rope attached and pulled the vehicle on to the bank. Mother-in-law was none the worse for her ordeal really – nowt that a large brandy wouldn't put right – but I think our hero gave up drink altogether. Well, for about a week maybe.

In my early peasant days The Happorths was always a grass field full of beef cows suckling their calves. Most of these bovine mothers were slow, lean, antique creatures and over the years had become remarkably tame. As soon as anyone entered the field they would gather round to have their backs scratched. If I was in a good mood – if the sun was shining, if there was nowt lyin' upside down, and if I was alone – I might well pause awhile and pass the time of day with some canny old cow.

On one bright morning I was met just inside the gate by a particularly friendly old Hereford lady who seemed to enjoy having her face rubbed. We had an ongoing joke, she and I, and on such occasions I would put my hands over both her eyes and say something like "Mind, I tell y' what, bonnie lass – the nights are cuttin' in sharp, don't y' think . . . ?"

You can imagine what a wholly ridiculous picture this would present to any unsuspecting observer – a fully-grown bloke in broad daylight trying to persuade an old cow it was dark already. I fear the next-door farmer, who just happened to be strolling by at the time, never really took me seriously after that little episode.

The field in front of the farmhouse is called the Front Field (well, what else would you call it?). At its highest point lies the site of an ancient settlement. To be honest I had no idea it existed until a professor from Newcastle University called and asked if he could excavate. He produced aerial photographs which clearly showed signs

80

of some pattern just below the surface, and his students began to carefully scratch away on a two-acre plot in early May. I was much younger then, and remember thinking the delightful female students crawling about my field on dimpled knees were a lot more interesting than any old bones they were ever likely to unearth. It was a splendid summer that year, and my entire staff (a canny lad) and I, worked diligently making hay all around the site. No hay was more thoroughly teased and turned and wuffled. I believe it was the sweetest hay we ever made . . .

Anyway, by September the band of nubile archaeologists had uncovered the remains of a small village. There was evidence of about a dozen round huts, each with a stone floor and signs of a fire in the middle. There had been a defensive ditch circling the houses, and beyond that an enclosed cobbled yard where livestock were probably secured at night. The diggers found tools, weapons, jewellery, all building up a picture of the folks who lived over there in the Front Field ages ago. In fact, Professor Jobey concluded these early peasants were shepherding their flocks long before the Romans arrived.

It would be a good place to live, I imagine – the river at the bottom of the hill, good grazing for their animals, enough timber to build their houses . . . and until that first centurion keeked his heed ower Shaftoe Crag, not a foreigner in sight.

The Tale Of The
One-Eyed Sideboard

AT the far side of the arena at Rothbury Mart there are two gateways leading out to the cattle and sheep pens. The animals enter the ring through one of these, and having been auctioned, leave by the other.

Overhead on the wall is the following verse:

Good luck to the hoof and the horn
Good luck to the flock and the fleece
Good luck to the growers of corn
With blessings of plenty and peace.

It sounds like a toast to all peasants, doesn't it? Glasses raised at the end of a farming year, the beginning of the next . . .

"Here's hopin' most of your auld mule yowes survive bonnie lad, and y' mek a bob or two . . . cheers!"

I met a retired farmer recently who remembers driving his sheep to this mart many years ago, before wagon transport. Just himself and a couple of collie dogs, gently shepherding perhaps two or three hundred lambs down from the hills to the big autumn sale. As he got nearer the town he would see his pal Willie with another flock away to the right, and Charlie coming down on the left. That would be Arthur over there shouting at his dogs, trying to keep his sheep together: "divvent hurry them . . . no use gettin' them t' the mart haff knackered . . . they've got t' look fresh 'n' fit in the ring."

From early morning there were lambs converging on the mart from most of the farms roundabout – moving, floating, rolling down the slopes, like advancing white battalions surrounding the town, coming in from all directions – a whistle, a bleat, a bark, carrying on the September air. I imagined there might be one hell of a mix up when all these different flocks homed in on the mart, but this fella said there was seldom much bother, and if Charlie ended up with a few of Willie's sheep the lads would soon sort them out in the pens. Everybody 'kenned' their own sheep.

It was a very important day in the farming year. No more than a few minutes in the ring for the sheep farmer to make his money. He often had nowt else to sell – the lambs were his harvest, his only real income. When he set off to walk home again at night, with just the dog for company this time, the mart cheque in his pocket would have to keep him and the missus (and the dog) for another twelve months.

Of course the mart didn't just sell lambs. It was always a venue for the buying and selling of cows and yowes and store cattle – and occasionally second-hand furniture and assorted domestic items. A few years ago we decided to 'let' an empty farm cottage, and I set off for Rothbury mart to purchase the basic ingredients. By mid-afternoon we had a well-worn bedroom suite, a table, some chairs, and a canny looking old fashioned sideboard with two drawers over double cupboards, nicely polished wood, carved legs, fancy knobs. After I'd paid the bill and loaded everything onto the pick-up, I tied it all down with baler twine, and set off for home, satisfied I'd done a canny job. Over the moors past the Forestburn Gate, through Scots Gap, and half an hour later drove carefully into the farmyard. Disaster, there was a drawer missing out of the sideboard.

Well, you can imagine a two-drawer sideboard with only one drawer in place leaves a ruddy great black hole where the other one should be – it just doesn't look well. I mean you can't put anything in there – the sideboard just stares at you with a pained expression, and a vacant eye. It was as much use as a clock without an hour hand, a wheelbarrow without the wheel.

So where on earth was this wayward drawer? It had to be found. Obviously nobody steals a drawer – it must've been lost on the journey home – slid out on a corner somewhere between here and the mart. There was no time to lose, only two hours of daylight left, so I ordered two bewildered offspring into the back of the pick-up (one on each side) and began the slow systematic search of verges and ditches all the way back to Rothbury. The kids freezing, complaining, and peering unenthusiastically into the hedgerows.

Along the route perplexed peasant folk came out to see what was going on. "What's going on?" they demanded.

"Y' haven't seen a drawer, have you?" says I sheepishly.

"A drawer?"

"Aye, a drawer – we've lost a drawer out of the sideboard."

At this simple explanation worried women would draw their children closer, protectively. Men with no-nonsense expressions emerged from behind the byre and looked aggressive. Who was this loon cruising about the byways supposedly looking for a sideboard drawer?

"What makes y' think we've got your bloody drawer?" they asked. "We've got all the drawers we need!"

"No, you don't understand," I protest, "y' see we had it at Rothbury mart, but it must've escaped somewhere along the road . . . ." But by then they'd all gone indoors and drawn the curtains.

We scoured every yard of the journey, concentrating on one side all the way there, and t'other side all the way back. There was no sign of a fugitive drawer, and now it was dark already.

Next morning I phoned the mart office. "Ah, I believe you've lost a drawer." said the secretary as soon as I told him my name.

"How did you know that?" says I.

"Well, everybody from here to Scot's Gap knows you've been wanderin' about lookin' for it." He was sniggering.

"Did I leave it at the mart?" I asked. "Have you got it there?"

"No," he says, "but I know where it is!"

Apparently a shepherd from up Greenleighton way had been checking his stock that evening and came across the thing lying in the dyke back. Now some people might've just left it there, ignored it. Others might've taken it home and used it as a tool box, or put a few hyacinths in it, or even chopped it up for kinlin. But not this bloke. He immediately sees the tragic significance of a one-drawer sideboard, and aware there'd been a furniture sale at Rothbury that very day, he put two and two together, and phoned the mart. What a man! I took him a bottle of whisky and retrieved the drawer. It was none the worse for its ordeal, and we've still got the sideboard.

More recently I attended another such auction at the same place, but this sale was a bit special. This was definitely not an occasion for newly-weds setting up home, looking for cheap sofas, odd chairs, bric-a-brac and

84

bargains. This time the ring area (where on other days suckler calves scuttled and skittered about) was piled high with the most beautiful furnishings from another age. Writing desk, book case, bureau, stately grandfather clocks – rosewood, mahogany, inlaid, veneered, polished, cared for. Bowls and dishes from the orient, teapots and music boxes, jugs and mugs, a sea of silver cutlery, an ocean of antique ornamental artistry. All this and more from one farmhouse tucked away down a quiet lane in the back of beyond, where a bachelor farmer with an eye for beautiful things had gathered this treasury about him. By the time he died I doubt if there was space for his wellies.

So we crowded in on this bleak wintry Wednesday – the curious (like me), the wheeler dealers, the amateur collectors, the well heeled and the dreamers. They'd viewed the goods, made notes, checked the building society account and now, armed with glossy catalogue, they parked thermalised bottoms around the ring and up into the gallery. There were rural ladies in Barbour coats and hair-does that wouldn't move in a force ten. They sat with stern concentration, not to be trifled with or diverted. And dealers from far afield, with just an air of roguishness about them, scribbling secret codes in black-backed notebooks, bifocals on the end of byzantine noses. Everyone seemed well prepared for a long day. Lots of thermos flasks, smoked salmon sandwiches (with the crusts removed!). The odd bottle of chilled Sancerre together with long stemmed glasses . . . a copy of The Independent for the long wait to lot 632 (or whatever).

It was relatively easy for the auctioneer – it was all high class stuff and the congregation willing and eager. Bids came readily enough. Occasionally he would even turn his back on the audience and take another fifty quid from a telephone behind him in the office. "You're out over there mind," he'd say, "my bid's on the telephone . . . all done? . . . It goes then." Bang. "Seven hundred pounds to the telephone." Who the phantom phoner was is anybody's guess . . . our man at Sotheby's? Lovejoy perhaps?

It was noticeable these people didn't bid like the farmers who frequent the more traditional livestock sales. Peasants tend to bid furtively: the merest hint of a wink, a raised eyebrow, a finger that barely moves, a glance, a twitch, a flinch. Not this lot. They waved their arms and catalogues with immodest enthusiasm, as if frantically trying to catch the eye of their aged granny who's just come through customs at Gatwick.

And of course there wasn't the incessant noise as on normal mart days – no anxious bleating, no bewildered blaring, no agricultural abuse from frustrated farmers – and no clarts.

"Well now," says the man with the gavel, "here's a very nice piece," and one of his henchmen holds up a double handed chamber pot – while munching a beef sandwich. The potty races to £150 in less time than it would take to make use of it.

"Now then look here, a very very nice item, lot 386" (must be something special – two 'verys' this time). It's a pair of 19th century marble lion figures, no bigger than a pair of shoes – and they break the two thousand barrier. A couple of silver candlesticks make five hundred, an ebony music box fetches twelve fifty. A bonny bowl with Chinese origins (big enough for a few bulbs maybe) goes for fourteen hundred. I know little or nothing of antiques and objets d'art, but prices didn't suggest any serious recession in the Rothbury area. Even the little fiddly things sold well. A wee wooden stool, the kind somebody might once have sat upon to milk a cow, made about seventy quid. Ye gods, I remember buying the cow for less – mind it was a while ago – and she was an antique cow.

Worse still, a brass dog collar went for two hundred and seventy. No self-respecting collie I've ever known would've been seen dead in it. A telescopic toasting fork made a hundred and fifty (obviously no mod. des. res. should be without one, even if they've only got central heating). A Grace Darling mug at eighty five pounds! Fancy dropping that on the kitchen floor as you took your cocoa to bed.

I left before the real classy stuff came up, and I suspect it would be well after dark before the professionals fought it out for that 17th century mahogany bureau, and pushed it into five figures. When I got home and looked around it all seemed 'very very ordinary' – not a Carmichael or a Canaletto to be seen. No marble lions on the mantelpiece (just a clock that hasn't worked for years, stuck at half past three). Not a proper 'objet' anywhere which, come to think of it, is maybe just as well. At least there's nowt worth pinchin'.

However, looking back at the sale, I think the mart could well add a few lines to that "prayer" above the gateways in the ring – if only to accommodate their expansion into the 'Antiques Mart Show'. How about:

Good luck to the Rosewood veneer
To the dealer with modest ambition
Good health to the poor auctioneer
Who struggles through life on commission.

'Unaccustomed As I Am . . .'

GEORDIE was working as a brickie up on the Roman Wall, somewhere beyond Haltwhistle, when he was arrested for thumpin' a centurion. Hadrian didn't mess about – no industrial tribunal, no trade union appeal – the lad was promptly shipped off to Rome for the "Games".

So there he is, poor Geordie, barred up in a dungeon underneath the Coliseum, with a ravenous lion waiting for his bait upstairs in the arena. The full house screaming for blood – Julius Caesar and his cronies reclining in the posh seats, eating grapes and drinking wine.

When his turn comes, Geordie is dragged out into the blazing sun, and the big nasty lion is released from his cage. He gets his eye on Geordie and hurtles towards him, slaverin' and roarin' and gnashin' his teeth.

The beast is going flat out, no more than ten yards from his victim, when Geordie puts his hand up and shouts "Whoa, had on a minute!" The bewildered animal screeches to a halt, and Geordie calmly bends down and whispers something in his ear. Immediately the monster lion turns tail and tears back into his cage, shuts the gate himself, tremblin' and shakin' in a helluva state – petrified.

The emperor is completely flabbergasted – seen nowt like it – and sends for Geordie straight away.

"George," he says, "that was truly amazing . . . Of course you're a free man, y'can start walkin' back to Haltwhistle whenever y'like – but tell me, what on earth did you say to the lion?"

"Well," says Geordie, "I just told 'im he could eat me if he liked but he wouldn't really enjoy the meal, 'cos on an occasion like this he'd probably have to make a speech when he'd finished. It was enough to put him off his supper!"

Alright, so it's not the funniest joke you've ever heard, but it's spotlessly clean, and it gets me nicely into this subject of 'speechifyin'.

Making a speech is the most ludicrous, petrifying, paralysing activity ever invented by man. I wonder who thought of it first – it has to be some prehistoric politician, doesn't it? An early parish councillor perhaps; I bet at this very moment the bloke is proposing a toast at a Round Table barbecue in Hades!

It's just a form of showbiz of course, and most public speakers are probably frustrated actors. Once they get the merest whiff of an audience, they simply have to stand up and blather about something – anything – sewage disposal, badger baiting, EEC regulations on cucumbers, unmarried mothers, inner city parking, the golf club accounts. It doesn't really matter what. Lack of knowledge on the subject seldom inhibits these people.

And very quickly they acquire a reputation for it. Somebody to give a vote of thanks? Oh good, Arthur's here, he'll do it. A toast to the Mayor? Arthur's your man. A few words after the christening? Uncle Arthur, naturally. It's nea bother. In fact, Uncle Arthur will expect to be asked.

He'll have a little all-purpose speech tucked away in his waistcoat pocket – just in case. He loves it – it's a drug, a turn-on. Well, it must be. Why else would anyone expose themselves to such frightful risks? Most of us would rather face a whole tribe of mad, screaming, spear-wielding cannibals.

Of course our friend Arthur, confronted by the same murderous horde, would quickly get to his feet, give a little cough, and proceed to bore the paint off them with 20 minutes on ethnic violence. They'd probably still boil him for supper, but he'd feel a lot better about it.

However, for normal everyday cowardly folk, public speaking remains the ultimate terror – the humiliating nightmare in which you step trembling on to the podium, only to discover you've forgotten to put your trousers on, and all your inadequacies are revealed.

Do the Uncle Arthurs of this world never forget the punchline? Does his voice never disintegrate in mid-sentence from manly baritone to whining boy soprano? Does he never get a terminal itch in his left knee (or somewhere much more embarrassing)? Does his nose never dribble into his beard until it looks like a tropical rain forest? Do his glasses never steam up when he's hot 'n' bothered and render him totally blind? Does he never discover his fly's undone halfway through his amusing talk to a stunned W.I.? Or is it only me . . . ?

The first time I ever made a speech was in Alnwick Young Farmers' Club. In those far-off days, before teenage sex and Test Match Special, the Y.F.C. was about the only source of rural recreation available. I think it was either that or the Young Conservatives, and they were far too up-market for simple country lads.

Anyway, you know how it is when you first join any organisation – you just sit huddled in the back row, determined not to cough or break wind in case somebody asks you a question or gives you a job. Sooner or later, of course, you're trapped – there's no escape. Maybe you were trying to impress the bonny lass sitting next to you – perhaps the team is one short and desperate. You could be a hero – everybody's looking at you – and suddenly you hear yourself "volunteer".

88

We were a public speaking team of three, competing (I suppose) with similar terrified teams from other clubs in the county – Berwick, Belford, Tritlington, Hexham and the rest. Each team had a chairman, a speaker, and a vote of thanks.

I got the speechifying job – five minutes on any topic y'fancied. The subject would inevitably be agricultural and exceedingly dull. We hadn't a clue about anything else. "The Life Cycle of a Mule Yow" perhaps (five minutes would certainly be long enough for that), "Common Diseases of the Pig", "Rearing Calves", "Training a Collie Dog" . . . all gripping stuff, likely to hypnotise any audience.

Another youth, Mathew, was to do the Vote of Thanks, with a weird farmer's daughter called Barbara in the Chair. The trouble with Barbara was her intense relationship with a horse. She was horse-mad. Every spare moment was spent in the company of her gee-gee. She groomed it, brushed it, pampered it, and occasionally trotted round the countryside on the beast.

Consequently, she permanently reeked of horse. What's more, she always dressed for the horse – covered all over with hairy hat, hairy socks, hairy duffle coat and smelly wellies. What lay beneath this layer of hair was anybody's guess, and as far as I can remember nobody was all that interested.

Anyway, twice a week, in an upstairs room of the Nag's Head in Fenkle Street, we practised for our "glittering debut" – and got progressively worse. A few nights before the big event it dawned on us just how bad we really were, and serious panic set in.

It was a bit late of course, but we desperately needed some

professional guidance. So we invited the English teacher from the Duke's School to listen in, and suggest any improvements he might deem necessary.

"Are we as terrible as we think we are?" we asked naively.

"Oh yes," he said.

"Is there anything you can do for us at this late stage?"

"Well, not really," said he, "except perhaps one very simple suggestion."

"What is it?" we demanded. "We'll do it – anything – tell us please." By now the tortured trio were convinced a public disaster was imminent. We would be embarrassed to death, make complete fools of ourselves – bomb in a very big way.

"Well," he said, "you must realise you're putting on a sort of dramatic performance – there could be a sizeable audience there. The Gazette might send their star reporter and a photographer (he wasn't making us feel any better). So the least you can do is look presentable – tidy, clean.

"As it is, you are three of the scruffiest hicks I've ever set eyes on. You're a bleedin' disgrace!" We sat there speechless. "Especially you," he said pointing at poor Barbara, ". . . and you smell like an allotment!"

Well, the man had hardly filled us with renewed confidence, but Mathew and I took his advice and made a supreme effort to smarten ourselves up for the big night. It isn't easy when you're a gangly spotty youth, but we both turned up squeaky clean in shirt, tie and rural Harris tweed suit – hair brushed – immaculate.

We wondered if Barbara would appear at all. Maybe she'd already galloped off in a huff, never to be seen again. However, only minutes before our team was due to go on stage and amaze the assembled throng, she suddenly walked through the door of the hall.

For several seconds nobody recognised her. Then everybody began to turn round and stare at this vision. Barbara had obviously taken the criticism very seriously. Gone the hairy coat, the wellies, the "stable look". Now a mane of gleaming golden hair hung down her back. Someone had "sprayed on" a cheeky little black number, with a neckline plunging to the navel and the hem split to the hip bone. I seem to recall three strategically placed sequins. Bits of Barbara we'd never suspected were revealed, and the lady just sashayed on to the platform, followed by her two open-mouthed team members.

Now it so happened the judge that evening was a well-known old agricultural roué (who had better remain anonymous) and he couldn't take his eyes off her. I'm convinced he never heard a word of the dreadful speech. He probably missed Mathew's spluttering vote of thanks altogether – never noticed the shuffling, sniggering congregation – he just ogled the delectable Barbara, and promptly awarded us first prize!

What a triumph – you couldn't shut us up for weeks after that. Ask any of us for the time of day, and we'd give you a long-winded waffle on the meaning of life. It was just the kind of dangerous experience that persuades boring old farts to stand for the European Parliament – and Uncle Arthurs everywhere to "just say a few words".

Ghost Story

TRAVEL north towards Alnwick on the A1, beyond the Felton by-pass, past Newton-on-the-Moor, and turn right across the dual carriageway where the garage used to be at Hitchcroft. You're heading for the coast now, and about halfway between Shilbottle and Alnmouth you'll pass the spot where the pit village used to be.

I drive along this narrow road almost every week, and most times find m'self glancing over the hedge, and remembering how it looked. There's nothing there now, save what was once the colliery manager's house, and somebody's renovating that. Otherwise not a shred of evidence as far as I can see – just another field of corn waving in the summer breeze.

Chances are it'll be a canny crop – it always was a useful bit of land as I recall. A little on the heavy side perhaps, and hanging to the north, but it could grow a useful crop of wheat in a decent year. It's called the Middle Pit field. There's a Bottom Pit field on one side, and a Top Pit on the other, but Middle is where the Longdyke Colliery stood, just below the village of Bilton Banks. You might never have seen or heard of it, and now it's just a bit of half-forgotten history.

Of course, nearby Shilbottle was always famous for the quality of her coal. They used to reckon the auld King insisted on nowt less for the fires in Buckingham Palace or Sandringham – had a few bags delivered every Friday. However, what you maybe didn't know was that the first Shilbottle pit was sunk a couple of miles to the north, right in the middle of Longdyke Farm.

The shaft was dug before the First World War by the Shilbottle Coal Company. A three-and-a-half mile track took the tubs back and forth on an endless rope system to the N.E.R. depot at Alnwick. (It might've been levelled out by the plough now, but when I lived there, you could still see where the rails had run in the Tramways field.)

In about 1920 Longdyke pit was bought by C.W.S., who soon decided it was becoming obsolete. Within five years they were sinking a new shaft at Shilbottle Grange, with its own rail link connected to the main London-Edinburgh line, just south of Alnmouth – and that heralded the end for Longdyke.

The new pit prospered, and after the 1939-45 war, and nationalisation, the N.C.B. modernised and expanded it, eventually merging it with Whittle. At its peak Shilbottle and Whittle employed over a thousand men – produced an awful lot of very good coal – but Longdyke is where it all began.

92

The Longdyke pit stood in a little valley at the north end of Trobe's Dene, and as I write this I have a photograph (dated 1912) showing the winding gear, the tall smoking brick chimney, a muckle waste heap, and the houses of Bilton Banks standing halfway up the hill beyond.

Of course I never saw coal come out of that pit – I'm not that ancient – it was no more than an industrial ruin when I was a kid, abandoned to the rats. But we played cowboys and Indians among the tumble-down buildings, slithered down the mountains of shale. We dropped stones into the bottomless shaft, counting the seconds until they hit the water, and the crash came echoing back up again.

Bilton Banks, the old pit village, survived until the late fifties, and I remember that well enough. There were two streets stuck on the hillside. "The Lang Raa" (Long Row) had 19 houses, I think, and (you'll never guess) "The Short Raa" consisted of maybe eight or ten. There was another raa of solid stone netties standing proudly in between. I suppose over a hundred folk lived there at one time. In my youth, nearly all the men worked at the new Shilbottle colliery – biked there over the hill, along Threatmore Lane, already dressed for the job. The bairns walked over the fields, carrying their dinner, pinchin' a bagie on the way, to the primary school. I don't remember any school bus.

And the women? Well I suppose they just made the best of it – keeping the house tidy, possin' 'n' manglin', hangin' oot the weshin', puttin' up the man's bait, feeding everybody – and carrying water. Water was a major issue! There was no sanitation in the houses. A bucket under the bed maybe, but certainly no bathrooms, no flushing toilets, and no water. One solitary tap served the whole community!

I remember that tap well. It stood like some sacred idol, a 'totem tap', at the end of the raas. One cold water pipe stapled to the wooden post. Somewhere to gather, blather and gossip. The unlucky ladies who lived at the bottom of The Lang Raa had a lang walk. Two pailfuls at a time, carried back to the house, using a square wooden frame (it had a name, but I've forgotten it). It would be placed on the top of the pails, inside the handles. The carrier would then step into the frame, pick up the buckets, and this clever wee invention simply kept the load steady, no splashing, and away from the legs and the varicose veins.

Several trips a day were necessary. The man coming home from his shift needed a bath (no pit-head baths then). The water would be heated in the set pot at the side of the black kitchen range, and poured into a tin tub on the cleaky mat in front of the fire. She'd scrub his back likely – and any other bits he couldn't reach.

You could hear the pit hooter two miles away as it sounded the end of a shift, and a little while later the blackened bicyclists would appear coming down the hill, helmets and knee pads hanging from the handlebars, mucky and thirsty.

There was a little shop at Bilton Banks, selling baccy, tea, sweets, Tizer, sherbet dips, and a few other essentials of life. If you were very lucky, there might even be a little piece of sweet locust in amongst the sherbet.

And in the halcyon days there was the 'Rec'. The recreation room stood on the green, below the football pitch. It boasted a full-size billiard table, cards, dominoes, newspapers, magazines – and of course an open coal fire. Well at least that was one luxury everybody had – a roaring coal fire.

I think coal was free – or near enough. In fact one of the first jobs I had after leaving school was leading coal with a horse and cart from Shilbottle pit to the threshing machine at Longdyke. It would be Mr Thompson's big polished traction engine that drove the thresher, I expect. I can't recall how much coal the beast consumed, but we just turned up at the pit and got a cartload whenever it was required. Nea bother.

There are bubbles above m'head even now – shadowy images of Bilton Banks floating there. A boy on a bike delivering a telegram sometime during the war. Whose door would he go to? Nobody keen to take the message.

An old retired miner – I think his name was Bob Douglas, but I'm not sure. Anyway, he's sitting on a massive log up by the tap somewhere, chewing Condor bar, and telling me of his days in America. He'd gone off to Pittsburgh during the depression to find work over there. "Why did you go all that way?" I asked naively. "T'better m'sell of course," he said. He came back though.

Other names linger in the memory – Knox, Egdell, Wilson, Pattinson; "Tombo" Pattinson I remember as one of the canniest rogues you'd ever meet. Mind you, chances were you'd only meet him if you happened to be wandering about in the middle of the night. He'd be settin' rabbit snares somewhere.

Eventually an enlightened Coal Board and the local council moved everybody out to some modern housing estate in Shilbottle or Alnwick, presumably with taps and toilets inside. It had to be better!

I flitted from Longdyke at the May term 1958, having just experienced one of the worst lambings in living memory. The sleet and snow through that Easter weekend killed hundreds of sheep, and probably drove a few

94

shepherds crazy as well. A nearby farm had 70 twins in a field on Good Friday, and barely mustered 70 singles come Easter Monday. It was the sheep equivalent of the Somme, and the empty houses at Bilton Banks saved us from total disaster.

Nowadays I suppose most farms would have a vast empty grain shed available, and would simply push any vulnerable livestock inside in an emergency. But in those medieval days, hemmels were already full of cattle, pigs, hay – whatever. Even then, every other spare bit of shelter we had, every loose-box, lean-to, stable stall, was crammed with miserable ewes and lambs. What to do with those still out in the fields? If we couldn't get most of them under cover, they'd surely perish.

Well, I'll tell y'. For several days – until Mother Nature finally relented, until the sleet abated, till the dry breeze blew, till the sun struggled through again – every sheep we had spent those terrible few days billeted in The Short Raa at Bilton Banks. There were sheep in the kitchen, the front rooms, upstairs in the bedrooms, even the odd one stuffed into a netty. And most of 'em survived among the dust and debris, and peeling flowery wallpaper.

Yes, I often glance over the hedge and think about that wee pit village, but it's just a crop of barley now. It might be full o' ghosts though.

Haway The Lads

IT seems a long time ago now – that all too brief golden era of K.K. Remember? When Newcastle was the capital of the universe and top of the Premier League. When St. James' Park was a theatre of dreams come true. When week after week United won with style and a hatful of goals in front of a packed house.

I was one of the unfortunate outsiders who could never get a ticket, so some of us did the next best thing and went to watch the superstars in rehearsal. Can you believe it? Maybe a couple of thousand mad things like me watching a training session! Of course most of the names have changed since then (footballers flit about like agitated birds, migrating mercenaries) and a new dynasty rules now. But for a while you may recall 'The Toon' reigned supreme. Everybody wanted to see them.

Anyway the boss wasn't there the morning I turned up. "A long standing engagement on the continent," somebody said. Maybe he was signing another superstar. Perhaps he and the bold Sir John were buying Barcelona – who knows? Anything was possible.

Terry Mac was the man in charge that day, or so my small fat informant from Low Fell told me. He seemed to know everybody. 'Low Fell' had been a devout supporter through all those damp depressing seasons, when the fire at St James' Park did little more than smoulder, seldom burst into flames – sometimes almost went out. Occasionally a few bright sparks called Waddle, Jinkie Smith, Gazza and the likes, would briefly promise to rekindle the embers, but were all too soon blown away on boardroom wind. Earlier still his Dad had watched Bobby Mitchell waltzing down the wing. Little Ernie Taylor turning on a sixpence. Jimmy Scoular, he of the oak tree thighs, repelling all invaders. Supermac scoring with half the opposing team hanging round his neck. To a time when, legend had it, the manager simply shouted down a pit shaft for a centre forward, and up he'd come, blinking into the light, ready to score a hat-trick on Saturday afternoon, nea bother. To the greatest Geordie hero of them all, Wor Jackie – the pedigree whippet with wings on his heels.

Aye, those were the days when 60,000 religious fanatics turned out to worship in bleak midwinter, to watch eleven black and white idols kick a greasy ball about in the clarts. A heavy leather ball wrapped around a bladder. Watery Bovril and a terminal pie at half time. Heaven.

I remember being packed into the paddock for a cup tie one day, when the vast crowd swayed violently like a wave, almost knocking over a noisy little fella standing next to me. "Wat 'ya pushin' me for?" he demanded angrily. "Couldn't help it," says I, "59,998 other folk are pushin' ME!"

He didn't seem at all convinced by this explanation, but his attention was diverted when the opposing centre half appeared to handle the ball in his own penalty area. "Hand baal!" he shouts, along with several thousand other voices. Immediately a cloth cap in front turns round and says, "git away man, he nivor touched it." "What? nivor touched it?" says m' stroppy neighbour, "Y' must be blind – the bugger had the laces oot twice!" Twice y' understand.

But the wilderness years lasted a long time, flashes of hope doused by disappointment, until just when it seemed oblivion beckoned, and even bankruptcy keeked over the main stand – came the Messiah. In fact two of them really. Hall and Keegan, a double act to rebuild a temple.

Three dramatic seasons on, and Newcastle were suddenly so successful you could hardly see them. Not unless you were into 'Bondage', had a Platinum seat, a corporate cubicle or a satellite dish. So that's why I found myself at this Monday morning training session in Durham. I figured this might be as close as I'd ever get to the new heroes.

Mind you, it still wasn't easy to get in. For a start I had to push my way through the 'guard of honour' at the main entrance. The posse of starry-eyed kids should possibly have been doing arithmetic at Framwellgate Moor Primary, but they'd sneaked away to meet their gods armed with sick notes and autograph books.

"Sign m' T-shirt man, will y?" – and Mr Ruel Fox, a dark skinned fleet footed winger, smiled and scrawled something totally illegible on the off-white vest he was offered. In fact anyone who looked remotely like a footballer was invited to sign something, before he disappeared inside to change for work.

The big names arrived in big cars. McDermott in a sober Rover, Barry Venison glided up in a much sleeker sexier machine – low and black. Lesser mortals – apprentices, juniors, those on trial – tumbled out of a club coach humping holdalls and cool boxes of Lucozade. Almost fifty players and staff were there.

It was a restricted area inside the building, but I strode purposefully after the players towards the changing rooms, trying desperately to look like an intrepid reporter. This is not easy for an ageing peasant. Maybe I should've worn a dirty trench coat and battered trilby – or did that go out with Humphrey Bogart?

A real reporter, our man from the Chronicle (with proper press credentials) was talking earnestly with assistant manager Arthur Cox. I suppose he needed a story, any story – he had a deadline, had to phone in something truly breathtaking to catch the early edition. Perhaps he got a scoop on Robert Lee's knee, or someone else's hamstring. Meanwhile the soccer paparazzi, loaded down with complex cameras the size of anti-tank weapons, hovered – waiting for a careless god to pick his nose. The noise from the changing rooms was of laughter, silly jokes, cheerful banter in a babel of languages and dialects. Spirits were high.

Chronicle man was now crouched furtively in a corner, pouring out 'instant deathless' to Sandra on the sports desk. "2.5 million new boy Kitson could stake a claim for Wednesday's Coca-Cola confrontation with Barnsley . . ." He was almost whispering, as if it was the latest scandal from the Palace.

However suspicions about me were mounting. I was getting some funny looks. Who was this mystery man? Could he be a spy from Blackburn Rovers, perhaps? An agent about to tempt a superstar? A hand alighted on my shoulders. "Excuse me sir, but have you some form of identification, a press card, written authority from the management . . .?"

I was about to come up with some blarney about an in-depth article for the Tow Law Bugle – another desperate deadline to meet, anxious editor sweating at his desk, that sort of thing – when I was saved by the players.

They came clattering out of the locker room, down the passage, and out into the rain. It seemed a good idea to follow them.

Outside a young coach took charge of the junior brigade, the budding Clarks, the embryonic Beresfords. Senior coaches went off with the first team squad, and a gaggle of goalies began a leaping and diving routine with a veteran called John Burridge. Barry Venison, golden locks falling over sweating tan, stayed indoors with the wounded, and at great speed went nowhere on an exercise bike.

In the pouring rain the players were stretching and sprinting, short sharp bursts, quick turns. The goalkeepers back peddling to turn high balls over the bar . . . diving one way then another without respite for point blank saves on the ground. They were all covered in mud. Later when everybody was thoroughly warmed up, the coaches rehearsed set-piece situations, ball control, quick accurate passing movements. I suppose similar scenes were being enacted at other clubs up and down the land, but this was Newcastle United, and we were top of the league. When did that last happen?

There'd been a minor miracle here, and maybe not so minor come to think of it. After all, it wasn't only the diehard football nut who'd been uplifted by the revival, it was most of the north east region. The whole area felt better I think. It probably functioned better. It had to be good news. Alright, alright – I know football is hardly the most important aspect of life on earth, not really – not like a nice warm bottle of Rioja, a crisp five iron hit stone dead in front of the clubhouse, or a cup of cocoa with Kim Basinger – but the cold northern winter was surely much more bearable with the Toon on top.

As I was walking back to the car, wet feet, freezing cold, runny nose, a Czechoslovakian goalie came jogging past looking warm and fit. "Good morning," says he, as bright as any Geordie spuggie, "Wattaday!" He was obviously feeling good, and why not? He'd had a clean sheet on Saturday – two nowt away to Aston Villa. Through the gymnasium window I could see Barry still toiling on his bike. It's not ALL glory – especially for a 'Geordie God' with a groin strain.

Pastoral Symphony

A WELL-KNOWN 'entertainer' was writing in the holiday section of the Sunday paper. He'd been all over the world – America, the Far East, tropical islands, snowy mountains, posh hotels, Italian villas. He'd been everywhere man.

Each year his band plays at the Edinburgh Festival, and for that week he's found a little hideaway in Northumberland. "Couldn't be better," he says. But he wouldn't reveal exactly where it was, in case somebody else finds it too.

Obviously no fool this chap – indeed, I have the same fears myself. It occurs to me there's a great danger that some eager, impressionable townie traveller from foreign parts could get completely carried away by the idyllic pictures we often paint of our rare fair county.

He might so easily be seduced by bonny photographs of the Coquet valley, intoxicated by lyrical images of the Cheviots, persuaded that Scot's Gap could be the very core of enlightened civilisation. He might even decide a quick flit from darkest suburbia to downtown Hartburn should be his next upwardly mobile move! Heaven forbid!

Of course, there's little doubt our Northumbrian countryside IS quite magnificent – no argument there. We all know about the crumbling castles, the ancient abbeys, the stately homes, the dark forests, the bright rivers tumbling down from rolling hills, the clear fresh air – and all that green romantic stuff. But steady on.

By all means let him come and have a quick look, but I suspect our idealistic urban immigrant wouldn't really have a clue what he was letting himself in for. Well, this is not the tranquil bucolic backwater it used to be, y'know. The pressures here can be quite frightening now – the stress almost unbearable (a social worker wouldn't last five minutes). In fact, I feel it's probably my duty to warn folks of the terrible dangers lurkin' "oot bye".

Oh, sure enough there was a time when the countryside was quiet, the pace slow, the livin' easy – but not any more. You'll maybe not believe it, but for a start we're under constant attack from the entire NATO airforce. I suppose the politicians and generals would argue it's simply for our own protection. They have to practise low-flying sorties somewhere – pretend Netherwitton is Baghdad and the chairman of the parish council a stand-in for sinister old Saddam.

So those Lightnings or Tornadoes (I wouldn't know the difference) come howling over the hill no higher than a Charolais' eye. They're gone in

100

seconds of course – before you can duck they're way beyond Berwick or Carlisle – but the noise is deafening, terrifying.

If it was for real, they'd never need to waste any of their high-tech weaponry on the likes o'me. At that first thunderous screaming swoop I'd be waving m'off-white string vest in abject surrender. Enough!

Then there's all that traffic at the end of the lane these days; it's continuous. I can remember when only a few tractors, the odd flatulent horse and Mr Batty's school bus ventured this far out, but not any more. On a bank holiday weekend it's like the M25, as a constant stream of Cavaliers and cream-coloured caravans heads west like an endless wagon train.

We country folk know better, of course. Public holidays are for tying up the gate with a piece of barbed wire, drawing the curtains and staying out of sight. My old neighbour on the next-door farm (he lived there from 1917-75) never even owned a car. He used Batty's bus occasionally, rode a bike or walked to the pub, got a lift to the mart in Telfer's wagon, felt he never needed a motor, and took nea harm. But that was yesterday.

And what about the bird scarers? Every peasant has at least one now – a sort of anti-crow artillery piece that bombards blanks into the battle zone above growing crops. Some days we're surrounded by them. Worse still, you can't always be exactly sure where they are.

Wander off for a quiet stroll along by Primrose Wood, deep in meaningful thought, at one with nature, maybe reciting a bit of Wordsworth to yourself – and one of these gas-fired howitzers cunningly concealed in the undergrowth suddenly goes BOOM – right up your trouser leg! It's not good for y'.

We shouldn't forget the Hunt either. You may not be aware of this, but once you sit somebody on a horse 16 hands above ground level, dressed in very tight jodhpurs and a hard hat, they feel obliged to shout and blow trumpets. They can't help it.

This in turn encourages the hounds to yap excitedly. The horses will then dance sideways across the road and leave large brown steaming deposits outside your new executive rural des res. Add to this the recent emergence of a weird army of 'saboteurs', ranting and raving and trespassing all over the place, on behalf of some smelly old fox (who's probably fast asleep in the next parish), and you can imagine the chaos.

And what's this? The 'shooters' are advancing from the Hall. Dressed like terrorists, armed to the teeth, and eager for the coming confrontation with the fiendish pheasant, they're unstoppable. Beaters are thrashing through the wood, petrified game is running in all directions (they've forgotten how to fly now). They try desperately to dodge the traffic on the Mitford straight – the poor things have little chance of course – and the B6343 lies carpeted wall t'wall with late unlucky birds.

Meanwhile, over the hedge, bewildered old sheep are bleating pitifully. Shepherds are hurling disgraceful obscenities at deaf collie dogs. Some peasant is spreading slurry (a bright golden haze on the meadow) upwind. Sex-crazed heifers are careering across YOUR lawn. Monster agricultural machines – bigger, brighter, noisier than ever – are roaring about the landscape, cultivating, combining and blocking the byways like new-age technicolour dinosaurs. Need I go on?

Alright, to be honest there are still a handful of rare quiet days in the countryside, but these are when the midgies attack. Robbie Allen would have you believe the real killers live up at Kielder, but they're ALL pretty lethal.

I remember we once had a little lass from Paris to stay. She came over on some sort of school exchange visit – never been out of the city, and the poor wretch didn't last long in rural Northumberland. However, when she first arrived, lost and forlorn at Morpeth bus station, I determined to greet her in her native tongue. Make her feel more at home, y'understand. Reduce the culture shock.

"Ah bonjour mademoiselle," says I (with perhaps the merest hint of a Geordie accent), "Honi soit qui mal y pense, toujours fromage."

She was naturally quite astonished, immediately assumed she'd been billeted with a bilingual peasant, and followed me all over the farm constantly blathering sixty t'the dozen, apparently unaware she'd already heard my entire vocabulary in her language.

One afternoon she followed me down the back field to see some cows and calves. It was a hot, still, steamy August day, and the herd was all in the shade, flicking their lugs and tails. I dunno – perhaps the attendant clegs and midgies got just a wee whiff of garlic or Chanel No. 5, but no matter – several million of them quickly abandoned the cattle and settled on petite Veronique. The poor kid was overwhelmed, fled in tears, pursued by a cloud of mam'selle-eating Northumbrian insects. She was covered all over in little bumps – pleaded to be sent home – claimed there were no flies like these in France!

Anyway, the message from all this friendly advice should be clear enough. Never assume for a moment that you'll find peace and tranquillity in today's countryside. Believe me, all those charming pictures are but a mirage. The din could drive you crackers.

I can just see that nice townie family parking the caravan for a quiet weekend, full of pure environmental thoughts and romantic notions – only to be buzzed by mind-blowing Phantoms, bombarded by a battalion of bird scarers, eaten alive by razor-toothed midgies, driven insane by wailing sheep, shot at by the gentry, hounded by the Seventh Cavalry, dunched by a giant tractor – and eventually, maybe just getting off to sleep, as our resident blackbird begins to tune his beak, at quarter past three of a summer's morning.

No, you'd never settle. Stay in Acacia Avenue, bonnie lad – it's much quieter there.

Rare, But Not Endangered

IT was the first time for me. I'd never actually seen them together in their lair. In pictures yes, on the telly of course, but never in the flesh, not LIVE! And yet there I was right inside their favourite habitat – watching, waiting – rather like David Attenborough in one of his excited whispering moods, as he creeps about in some slimy bog observing mating toads or whatever.

I have to tell you I'm no great authority on rare forms of animal life – not really. Once a modest knowledge of the mule yow perhaps, some experience with inadequate collie dogs, lean Friesian calves – but just your everyday farming stuff to be honest. Yet I knew this lot scuttling around before me now were definitely a bit special, unique even. Only 651 of them in the whole country!

"Good Lord," you cry, "is that right? Another endangered species – shouldn't they be preserved, protected from the big nasty polluted, high-tech, stress-laden world about them? Their days must surely be numbered!"

Huh, y'must be kidding. These creatures can look after themselves quite nicely thank you. In fact they're as safe as the Houses of Parliament – which is precisely where they congregate and blather. Have you ever been there? Have you ever wandered along those corridors of power and seen the history makers at play? It's well worth a visit, even if you're not a political animal. The actors may change, but the stage remains the same.

On my visit I duly reported at St Stephen's Gate, where a posse of large bobbies ensured there were no bombs about my person. Through the scanner, retrieve the car keys, three pounds sixty-eight pence in loose change, five fluffy old Polo mints – and we're into the cradle of democracy.

Immediately inside, there to the left, steps lead down into the Great Westminster Hall. It's 240 feet long and about 70 feet wide – clear span, vast high hammer-beam roof littered with carved angels. Built by William Rufus nearly 900 years ago (some of the original structure still remains) – this is a place where kings held council, where dark knights jockeyed for power. Where Thomas More lost his argument with Henry VIII in 1535. Where Charles I was tried and lost his head just across the road in 1649. He was the last sovereign to enter the Commons. Here in this hall Oliver Cromwell took the oath as Lord Protector; George VI and Winston Churchill lay in State.

It echoes with history, treachery, intrigue, law and disorder. I look at it in wide-eyed wonder, and what do I see (it's the simple peasant in me, I suppose)? I see a fabulous building for wintering cattle or storing barley! Well – it's high, cool, airy – and there are no awkward pillars to impede a muck-loader or a grain bucket. The biggest of Telfer's wagons would get in and out easily. I can picture it full of canny bullocks lying chewing the cud on clean straw of a frosty night.

But move on, you rural philistine – along St Stephen's Hall, a chapel once upon a time, the Commons sat here 450 years ago. On to the cathedral-like Central Lobby. This (as the name suggests) is the very core of the Houses of Parliament now, where all sorts of folk meet and patiently wait.

The Saints, George, Andrew, Patrick and David have been waiting here since the Palace was rebuilt after a great fire in 1837. (Apparently some clerks were burning a pile of Exchequer rubbish in the House of Lords' basement when it got out of control. The blaze destroyed the entire old medieval building, all except that Great Westminster Hall.)

Now statues of Gladstone, Russell, Granville and Northcote stand in pompous pose around this octagonal room. Paintings and carvings of royalty cling to high panelled walls, as today's parliamentary figures hurry by clutching important papers, earnest expressions on famous faces. "Isn't that wotsisname? Wasn't he once Foreign Secretary?"

And there I am too, an ordinary mortal lingering in this extraordinary meeting place, when out of those panelled walls emerge men in tail coats, knee breeches and white stockings. Something is obviously about to happen. We all freeze.

"Hats off for the Speaker!" cries a voice that demands attention, and along from her own special house on the north east corner of the Palace, overlooking the river, comes the delectable Betty Boothroyd. She's escorted by her 'officers', preceded by the Mace, and she looks like a queen. Smaller than I imagined (did I read somewhere she'd been a Tiller Girl? Are her legs really long enough for the chorus line?) No matter, the lady is a cracker, smiling and in complete control.

She passes right by me, and I have a tremendous urge to wink. I don't of course ("Into the Tower with the fool!") but she definitely nods very sweetly as she glides past to take her chair in the Chamber. I think, briefly at least, I must be in love – but it's reasonable to suppose the entire House is as well.

Commons business can't begin until the Speaker is in her chair, but the debating has already begun before we humble observers are allowed up into the Strangers' Gallery to peer silently down on those who control our lives and taxes. The Education Minister is at the despatch box answering probing questions on student loans, GCSE results, and little village schools condemned to die. A grand old Tory dame, a long-time fixture I suspect – smart suit, lots of jewels and lacquered coiffure – drones on far too long about education cuts in Bradford and Morecambe and Barnsley, before Betty loses her patience and puts a stop to it.

"The Honorable Lady must realise she cannot be allowed to leap back and forth across the Pennines all afternoon – enough. I call the Honorable Member for Bolsover."

The 'Beast' has been up and down half a dozen times already, but when eventually he gets his chance he doesn't mess about – he goes straight for somebody's jugular. While he's ranting, the Chamber is filling up. Edward Heath sails in and berths at his traditional mooring, oblivious of any storms raging about him.

Several other members appear to have their own special seats, but as Prime Minister's Question Time draws nigh, some are obliged to sit in the gangways or stand. There are only seats for 420 MPs. By the time the leaders enter, cheered into the arena like a couple of gladiators, the House is packed. It's all very theatrical, almost showbiz – and mercilessly adversarial.

The party leaders swap punches and insults across the despatch box, using the table to lean on or thump. There is a short sharp exchange on excessive executive salaries: "it's privatised greed, it's corporate gravy" (cheers for the question, boos for the answer).

The 'cash for questions' saga raises its head again. Stories of gifts and freebie trips abroad, nights in posh Paris hotels – even jars of honey allegedly given to innocent 'consultants'. Laughter and heartless jeers to embarrass the obvious culprits. You might conclude this is a bit of a pantomime, slap-and-tickle burlesque – but I'm assured real work DOES go on in offices, in corridors, over a cup of tea or a gin 'n' tonic, and often late into the night.

And all the time there's the constituency to 'nurse'. Back home the precious voter worries about his council tax, grandad's heating bill, cousin Walter's unemployment benefit. This little village wants street lighting,

106

that little village a by-pass. There's a Child Support Agency problem here, a rent dispute there.

Our man Alan Beith represents an area of 231,456 hectares (that's well over half a million acres) from Tweed to Wansbeck, from Alnmouth to Wooler and beyond, with about 55,000 voters scattered about the landscape. Three of the biggest parliamentary constituencies in England – Berwick, Hexham, Penrith and the Border – lie right along the boundary with Scotland, from sea to sea.

Four hundred years ago this was mostly reiver territory, bandit country, a no-go area, no law save that of an Armstrong, a Charlton, an Elliott or the likes. There are a few larger seats in Scotland of course, but Hexham (251,000 hectares) is England's biggest. Penrith comes second, Richmond in Yorkshire third, and Berwick fourth. As you can imagine, the voters in these far-flung outposts are thin on the ground – mostly peasant folk, village people, fishermen. Hexham has a 58,000 electorate, while little urban Newcastle Central has more than that packed into a few crowded housing estates.

But enough of speeches and statistics. It was Westminster's quiet stones that left the lasting impression . . . the wonderful architecture. I don't really know if the building is still functional in this day and age, but by God it LOOKS good, inside and out.

What the rest of the world readily recognises (Big Ben, the Commons, the House of Lords – the lot) was designed by two men. After the fire destroyed most of the old mish-mash of buildings, a design competition was held, and the winner was a London architect, Charles Barry. He was joined by an artistic gentleman of French origin, one Augustus Welby Northmore Pugin – and between them they drew up the plans and supervised the building of the whole thing – the internal decor, and even most of the furnishings. It cost two million pounds to complete in 1870. Can you imagine what kind of concrete and glass disaster might be built today? And how it would be paid for?

I left the way I came in. Outside, Richard I waved from astride his horse, and Cromwell just looked thoughtful. Inside, the rare breed would still be blathering away, with bonny Betty keeping an eye on them all. "Order . . . Order!"

Born Too Soon

LAST night somebody phoned me from Alaska. Now you probably think that's no big deal. Alright, so your cousin Mildred is constantly ringing from Australia to tell you about her operation.

Perhaps you're a business tycoon, and talk to Hong Kong twice a day. Or maybe your daughter just called from Rio and reversed the charges. But for the likes of me – a simple country lad with no technical talents whatsoever – a telephone call from the other side of the world is still a breathtaking event. Absolutely amazing!

It's not that I imagine for a moment that Alaska might not have a telephone you understand, obviously they do – probably more than one. No, the incredible thing is that this fella sitting in the middle of Eskimo Nell country can pick up his piece of coloured plastic, punch in a few appropriate numbers – and within seconds my piece of plastic (hanging on our kitchen wall, umpteen thousand miles away) begins to ring, pleading to be picked up. I lift the restless creature from its cradle, and clear as a bell the man says "Hiya Henry, howya doin'?"

If that isn't magic, I don't know what is.

Of course, my generation can remember the days when we wound a wee handle and summoned up Elsie the local operator. "Could you connect me with Longhorsley double seven, please?"

"There's nobody in," she'd say. "They're all away to Rothbury Mart – won't be back until teatime – and they're out for supper tonight as well, but you might catch them about seven o'clock if you're lucky . . ." That woman knew everything, and everybody.

Well, I suppose that was pretty remarkable for its day, wasn't it? But now we're on our own. Elsie is long gone, of course. Today we pick up the receiver, poke the digits, and musical bleeps fly along the wire to a little brick building just down the road. In there (I understand) a collection of clever electronic gadgetry will dispatch your bleeps to a bigger, more complicated place miles away.

Somehow your bleeps are immediately sorted out from a trillion other bleeps: they're fired into space, bounced off a satellite, and end up in exactly the right house in Acacia Avenue, Tokyo (or wherever) in less time than it takes to blow your nose. Unbelievable!

And how on earth somebody can blather to his office or his girlfriend while sitting in a car using a phone that isn't even attached to anything is mind-boggling. In fact I've long since come to the disturbing conclusion that this world is progressing (if that's the right word) far too rapidly for me. All this high-tech sorcery is just too much.

But then to be honest, it always has been. Anything remotely mechanical, anything that combusts internally, drives pistons, flywheels or whatever – anything that boils, or lights up, or revolves at the flick of a switch – remains a total mystery. No use me tinkering with tappets or a spluttering carburettor, or a wayward washing machine. If the problem cannot be resolved by a violent blow with a large claw hammer, it's obviously much too complicated.

And now it's getting worse, I fear. The bold new bewildering world of science, technology and computerised thingummyjigs has sneaked up on the outside and simply passed by me. Probably while I was lambing a mule yow.

Take a car radio, for instance. Does anybody actually study that vast impenetrable operating manual that comes with it? What a complete bore – like some turgid Russian novel. Why can't we just twiddle a knob as in olden days? Now I'm forced to bribe some spotty ten-year-old to programme all those ridiculous controls so that Radio Four, Radio Five or Classic FM can be at my inadequate fingertips. That is until some heavy metal mechanic scrambles them all again in his search for Iron Maiden.

Which reminds me . . . The car is regularly serviced down beside the Tyne Tunnel somewhere, and the garage always loans me a replacement vehicle for the day. Sometimes it's almost new. On one terrible occasion I drove off in a smart little hatchback with virtually nowt on the clock. Luckily the gears and most of the other important bits seemed to be in the same place as my own car, so we got back as far as Morpeth without mishap. There, I parked outside the Town Hall and went off to do some shopping.

Half an hour later I came back and casually put a small parcel on the roof while I groped for the keys. Immediately all hell broke loose! Unknown to me, the cunning little beast had a thunderous alarm system fitted, and it wouldn't shut up. It was howling like a demented banshee!

"Can somebody tell me how to silence this thing?" I pleaded pitifully to anyone passing by.

"Nuthin' to do with us," they said. "If it's your car, you should know how to stop it."

A sizeable and suspicious crowd was gathering already, pointing and muttering – probably a few vigilantes among them, eager to hang this dodgy character from the nearest lamp-post. I felt I had to get out of town – now!

The bitch was still screaming as I reversed out into Bridge Street. The noise was deafening as I drove (scarlet with embarrassment, cowering beneath the dashboard) over the pedestrian crossing and up Newgate Street. Shoppers stopped to stare and point; some even waved. I just wanted to get out into the country, where hopefully only a few dozy sheep would recognise this idiot.

But it was a Wednesday (market day), and the traffic was heavy and progress painfully slow. I was obliged to follow a creeping bus with cruel mocking children gesticulating gleefully from the rear window. Most of the pupils at the Chantry School emerged to dance up and down with delight as I howled past. Bewildered dogs were barking everywhere.

On through sleepy Mitford and slumbering Hartburn, still shrieking a warning of approaching incompetence. They could hear me coming miles away. That 15 minute journey seemed to take all day, before I reached home and phoned the garage.

"Just press the little button on the key ring, sir," he said very quietly. He could barely conceal the derision in his voice.

It was not a good day, but you have to realise some of us were just born a bit too early for this fiendish nonsense.

And what about the video? Don't mention it – just when I think I've got that animal tamed, it leaps up and laughs at me. I believe it sits there silently smirking.

"Here he comes again," it whispers to the telly. "Look, he's got the instruction book in one hand and the little gadget thing in the other. He's got his specs on too – he must be serious. I bet he wants to record the golf on BBC 2. Tell y' what, we'll give 'im the omnibus edition of Neighbours instead – that'll get him really excited!"

Alright, I admit it – the box of tricks is far too clever for me.

And don't talk about computers and word processors. Oh, I realise they're brilliant inventions. I fully appreciate they can correct my

APPAWLING spelling, shuffle garbled paragraphs about the page, and probably even work out the quickest way to Alaska – but not if you have an absolute moron with an obsolete brain sitting in front of it. Ye Gods, it takes me long enough to write this rubbish with a pencil – the last thing I need is an intellectual 'mouse' dashing all over the screen rearranging the grammar.

And while we're on the subject, you can keep your fabulous fax machine as well. Go on, catch whatever swims into the Internet, wheel and deal with your barrowload of E-mail, but count me out. I'm not up to all this fancy modern witchcraft.

Look at it this way: what's the point of living quietly, hidden away in the back o' beyond, well off 'The New Information Highway', if every rep and salesperson on the planet can find you simply by pushing a few brainy buttons? I'll settle (reluctantly) for a second-hand answerphone and the postman. That's quite enough sophisticated new technology for me thank you. I haven't mastered the old barbarian stuff yet!

In fact I have to tell you that I'm not entirely sure which wire goes where on a three-point plug. Red used to be the live one, I think, but just when we got the hang of it, those damned Europrats went and changed all the colours, didn't they? Typical.

Even basic plumbing and joinery, or being what's known as "a

proper little treasure about the home", have never been talents that came easily. Of course I realise such faculties can save a fortune, but not if you're a DIY delinquent they don't. Putting up that useful little shelf in the kitchen could ultimately lead to major structural surgery to save the building. Better to leave it to the dedicated handyman.

I was once inspired to build a small box-like plinth with breeze blocks to support the farm's diesel tank. Now you'd think nobody could go far wrong with breeze blocks; they're big, they're uniform, they're oblong. All you need to get it right is a spirit level and a piece of string. Nothing simpler, I hear you snarl.

Well, maybe for a reasonably useful person, but this architectural miracle somehow ended up with a distinct lean into the prevailing wind. And it's only five breeze blocks high! No kidding, a blind man on a galloping horse would notice it straight away – and I see this ridiculous monument to my own incompetence every bleedin' day. I wish it would fall down some night, but I know it won't – because I poured in several cubic yards of concrete to keep it up.

Anyway, you might still be wondering why this bloke phoned from Alaska. Well I'll tell you – he and his canny wife have recently been over here on holiday. Now as you know, Americans usually do the quick cultural tour of Europe, and Hank and Alys (having never been to this side of the pond before) might well have settled for the delights of Vienna, Rome, Paris, and Madrid. However, after landing at Heathrow they decided the only place to be was Scot's Gap (no fools, these folk) and I got the job to shepherd them around.

It wasn't too difficult, there's plenty to see – the Roman Wall, Holy Island, Hexham Abbey, a dozen dramatic castles like – well, take your pick – Alnwick, Bamburgh, Warkworth. Better still, blooming rhododendrons at Cragside, the gardens at Wallington, or maybe just a gentle meander up the Coquet, the North Tyne, the Breamish – along winding country lanes with views to render even an American speechless (well, almost).

Thank the Lord some bits of the world are still <u>low</u>-tech. In fact no tech at all.

A Lovesome Thing

THERE may be fairies at the bottom of YOUR garden, but sadly WE just have a septic tank. Smelly fairies perhaps.

Naturally I've done m'best to conceal this beast, or at least camouflage it – a shrub here, a rose bush there, even a little low wall stuffed with bonny flowers – and indeed these things CAN sometimes confuse the casual visitor. That is until they linger too close, and begin to ponder on the unique fragrance floating about.

This garden was an abandoned wilderness when I first moved in. Once upon a time it had undoubtedly been cared for – produced taties and veg for the folks who lived in the cottage – but since then nettles, thistles, dockens, wickens and 'auld man's baccy' had all prospered. So what to do with it?

I'm no Alan Titchmarsh y'understand, but in this case the only sensible option was to burn off all the rubbish, and get back to square one. Of course that was the easy part. As soon as cultivations began, all kinds of buried treasure bubbled to the surface.

I remember bits of bike and pram, remnants of antique farm machinery, and rusty old horseshoes. (As you may know, one is obliged to spit on rusty old horseshoes, and hoy them over your left shoulder – for good luck.) And bones, thousands of bones! Any passing archaeologist might well have been persuaded this was some ancient Geordie burial site. But no – these were not the remains of Scot's Gap man, or a lost centurion, or even a persistent and irritating worm drench rep – just the skeletons of a few mule yowes (mid 20th cent.), a favourite cat who must've run out of lives, and a right good collie dog I buried myself, after Tommy Armstrong ran over the poor thing with the Fordson tractor, years ago.

So anyway, having dug it over, removed the debris and created a nice clean seed bed, what now? It was much simpler being a farmer – you simply sowed wheat or barley or whatever all over the place, in muckle big 30-acre blocks. The choice of crop was fairly limited, and you certainly weren't concerned with colourful patterns. What's more, if the harvest went well, you might even make a bob or two. With this wee garden project, the only return would be a bad back.

In hindsight we should've commissioned some green-fingered guru to plan the job properly – someone with enough imagination to conjure up "a lovesome thing God wot". But instead, predictably, I hurriedly pressed in a barrowload of pinks and pansies and primulas, planted a couple of

114

flowering shrubs, a lone laburnum, scattered some grass seeds – and before you could say "aren't the nights cuttin' in already", we had a rather dull, instant garden. And that's how it remains – neat enough, I suppose, but obviously cobbled together without much thought or patience. And you can't get away with that. Mother Nature will not be hustled by a hasty horticulturalist.

Which brings us to the master gardener himself, who (as everybody knows) was born just up the road from here. Now there was a man with extraordinary patience, and an inspired imagination that stretched way beyond his own lifetime!

Lancelot Brown was the son of farming folk who lived at Kirkharle. The family had earlier moved from Ravenscleugh in Redesdale, and his uncles Henry and George also farmed at nearby Mirelaw House and Shielhill. His parents William and Dorothy produced three boys and three girls – Lancelot was number five child, baptised on August 30, 1716.

There was a village school at Kirkharle in those days, and presumably the children would go there for starters, but sometime later Lancelot certainly attended the school in Cambo. It was an establishment with a very good reputation, and by the time he left at 16, he was a lad with "a fertile and ingenious mind", and a clear picture of what he wanted to do.

His elder brother George (who married a Hartburn lass) was back on

115

the farm by now, but Lancelot went to work for the local landowner, Sir William Loraine, and it was this gentleman who gave our hero the start he needed. Success in most things is often a matter of just being in the right place at the right time, isn't it? And then grabbing the chance of course.

Lancelot was in the right place. A bright young man, brought up among the natural delights of the Wansbeck valley, fascinated by the architecture and gardens of big country houses (he would pass Wallington Hall every day on his way to school) and now under the wing of someone with considerable influence, about to re-shape his own estate. It sounded like the right place.

The timing wasn't bad either. This was an era when grand houses with expansive grounds were being created or improved throughout the land. What's more an earlier fashion for formal geometric garden design was being replaced by a broader, softer, more pastoral look. Perhaps not so much up here in darkest Northumberland; not yet. This far-flung outpost had for too long been a land of battlefields, castles and pele towers – but a little further south there were some dramatic changes afoot. In Yorkshire, Sir John Vanbrugh had recently built Castle Howard for the Carlisle family, described as 'The Top Seat and Garden in England'. Nearer home the same architect had been involved with work at Lumley Castle and Seaton Delaval.

And we were now at the beginnings of the Agricultural Revolution as well. A farmer in Norfolk called Charles (Turnip) Townshead was perfecting a four-course rotation for crops that would transform farming. Jethro Tull at Prosperous Farm in Berkshire (a dangerously optimistic name for a farm) had invented a seed drill which allowed plants to be sown at regular spacings – so making it easier to hoe the crop and control weeds. The first real leap into farm mechanisation. Jethro even produced a book in 1731 (Lancelot left school a year later) with the enthralling title 'The New Horse-Hoeing Husbandry – Principles of Tillage and Vegetation'. I doubt if it was ever a best seller – it may never be made into a movie starring Hugh Grant – but I wouldn't be surprised if Lancelot read it sometime in his career.

And another thing . . . There was a whole lot of very serious money sloshing about at this time. The Empire was booming, Britannia ruled the waves, fortunes were being made. Stately homes were springing up all over the landscape. For instance, Robert Clive came home from his adventures in India with more money than he knew how to spend – and

116

promptly purchased a mansion in Berkeley Square, and THREE country estates. Yes, all things considered, these were exciting times for rural England, especially if you had the right connections. (So what's new?)

Meanwhile, Lancelot's boss, Sir William, probably inspired by all this activity in the air, had embarked upon a major improvement of his own Kirkharle property. The large country house was 'modernised', the formal layout of the grounds completely redesigned, well over half a million trees planted, the church extended – and just to show he wasn't fiddling about, the entire village was moved to higher ground!

It was in this tumult of change that the bold young Brown served his apprenticeship, learned the fundamentals of land reclamation, drainage, horticulture and building construction. Although still only a relatively callow youth, he was entrusted very early with transforming a particularly unattractive stretch of boggy ground to the north of the house.

He must have done a canny job. Sometime later John Hodgson wrote: "over this he contrived to throw the sweetest charms, and convert the landscape into a woody theatre of stateliest view". Alright, I realise that sounds somewhat lyrical for these cynical days – but it was Lancelot's first piece of rural artistry, and it obviously caught the eye.

Work on the Kirkharle estate was completed in 1738, by which time the reputation of Sir William's gardener had already spread about the region, and he was even taking on several local commissions. But Lancelot was an ambitious young man, and a year later he decided to try his luck down south where the real action was. Armed with letters of recommendation from the Loraine family (Sir William had represented Northumberland in Parliament, Lady Loraine's father was a High Sheriff of Bucks) he took employment with Lord Cobham at Stowe. At first he worked under the watchful eye of a renowned architect and garden designer, William Kent – a man who certainly guided and influenced this newcomer from the North. Lancelot was still only 24.

By 1741, with a mixture of good fortune (the old head gardener left, the steward hanged himself) and some very impressive work, he had quickly risen to take over both their jobs, and was in charge of all the grounds, acting as paymaster and responsible for a staff of 40.

Once again Lancelot had chosen the right place to be, and his timing was perfect. Lord Cobham was not only ready and eager to make changes on his estate – he was also at the very heart of English aristocratic life, a friend or relative of almost everybody in high society. The many distinguished visitors who came to Stowe obviously saw Mister Brown's work, and as his reputation grew he was in great demand, often loaned out by his master to rearrange the grounds of other well-heeled households in the region.

And young Lancelot had another great gift, it seems. Our man could wheel and deal and chat with anybody, no matter who they were. I imagine he could be duly deferential to his illustrious patrons when necessary – remove his cap at the dinner table, tug his forelock occasionally, know when to say nowt, that sort of thing. But apparently his immense practical know-how, an ability to get things done, and a healthy disdain for footling officialdom, all combined to make him the man for the job. Very often he became a close personal friend of those he worked for – including King George.

Cobham died in 1749, and soon afterwards Lancelot decided to set up on his own. Croome in Worcestershire, owned by the Earl of Coventry, was his first major commission. Here he acted as architect, designer, drainage engineer, builder – the lot. He designed the splendid mansion as well as much of the interior work, and re-shaped the surrounding grounds in his own particular natural style.

The rest is history, or at least an important chapter of English history, littered with permanent memorials to Lancelot (Capability) Brown, the farmer's boy from Kirkharle. There's Blenheim of course – perhaps his most famous work. The Royal Gardens at Richmond, Broadlands in Hampshire (his bill for that job was £20,000), gardens and lakes at Syon House, the parklands at Alnwick Castle, a massive development at Burghley in Lincolnshire, a small lake at Rothley – and many others.

Some time after Brown's death in 1783, Lord Coventry, grateful for a stretch of tranquil countryside his old friend had created, erected a wee statue by a path to a pond. The inscription reads: "To the memory of Lancelot Brown who by the powers o' his inimitable and creative genius formed this garden out of a morass".

That, of course, was the man's greatest talent – and that's how he acquired his nickname. He could SEE the capabilities of the morass, and fashion there a picture that would still look good several lifetimes later.

I fear my little instant plot, with its scenic septic tank, may have to be redesigned long before that.

All The World's A Stage

LONG ago some betwitched auld grandad turned to his missus and said: "Well, pet, if we'd known the grandchildren were gonna be so canny, we might've had them first . . ."

What he'd discovered of course is that (unlike one's own kids) these delightful smelly little creatures only intrude upon your dull, predictable, comfy routine in short, sharp, quite acceptable bursts. They come for tea. If you're not concentrating, they may even stay a whole weekend – but then allelujah – they go away.

You might visit them for Sunday lunch perhaps, play games, read them daft stories about giants and hedgehogs, but always confident in the absolute certainty that come bedtime you'll be long gone. It's easy: someone else will wipe the snotty nose or (worse still) the other end. Somebody else will mend the wounded knee, the tortured tummy, cope with the petulant whinge, get up in the middle of the night to slay monsters, dispense sticky cough medicine – get them to the loo on time.

This is the stage in life – I suppose it's somewhere 'twixt Shakespeare's "eyes severe . . . beard of formal cut" and "second childishness . . . mere oblivion" – when grannies and grandads wear kind, understanding smiles, display quite uncharacteristic tolerance, mutter lots of oohs and aahs, and say things like "ee mind, he's a real divil, isn't he?" knowing full well they would've kicked the corn flakes out of the little sod in their day.

But that, of course, was a different day, in a very different world. You may well have "been there, done that" half a dozen times, but it was much simpler then. Oh yes it was. Well, for a start there was no such thing as political correctness to confuse and dilute traditional common sense.

There were certainly far fewer distractions available (at least in rural Northumberland) and as far as I can remember, no instruction manuals from some 'enlightened' government quango on how to be a proper caring parent. Indeed, looking back, I can't believe anybody could've been so unprepared or naive as m'self. Ye gods, I barely understood the procedure that induced the parental condition, let alone the problems that followed! But we managed.

Now, "in lean and slippered pantaloon, spectacles on nose", memories of that exciting time tend to be conveniently coloured or corroded. Yesterday's filters are thoroughly bunged up, and the plugs only spark intermittently. Early years of fatherhood, and the subsequent patter of tiny wellies, are little more than a cloudy soup, seasoned by occasional bizarre recollections of the chauvinist peasant struggling to pay the rent.

Oh, of course there are photographs somewhere of bonnie bairns feeding an orphan lamb, or seated on a tractor grinning at the camera, cuddling the dog of the day – but seldom with me. I tell myself (but perhaps it's just another inadequate excuse) that fathers simply didn't get involved in those days. I can still conjure up images of "shining morning faces" creeping unwillingly to catch Batty's school bus – but through much of that first "muling and puking" stage, I think I must've been very busy down the back field.

But then came the teenager. Now teenagers have probably always been a troublesome bunch – even my timid generation. In fact every generation since Cain and Abel, I suspect. Unco-operative, moody, expensive beasts, and generally far too complicated for simple grown-up folk. Especially the girls. Well at least the fellas are more or less predictable, aren't they? They just do silly straightforward damage – like drink too much beer, throw up on the landing, and wreck your car.

Obviously this can be rather disappointing, but it's the lassies, those lovely wee creatures with melting giggles and ankle socks, who suddenly blossom (overnight it seems) into smouldering nymphets, acquire persecution complexes, terminal acne and bras! And before you know it, there's an army of spotty youths yomping out from the city to deflower them! I expect mother had the appropriate chat with the little darlin's at the time, but naturally I was far too embarrassed –

and anyway by the time they were thirteen, they undoubtedly knew much more than I did.

No, my job was to find them, and bring them home after the weekend orgies at the rugby club. There, in the early hours of the morning, I would join a whole battalion of bleary-eyed parents, way past their own bedtimes, sitting in dark cars (fag ends glowing) all waiting impatiently for Sandra, Dawn, Carol, or whoever to emerge from the bushes, dishevelled, smiling sweetly – and wide awake!

Once you got them home however, they could sleep for England. Nothing kips like a well-raved teenager. They must need it, I suppose, to replenish their hormones – but often the first indication they might still be alive on a Sunday would be some tuneless din, playing at a trillion decibels, coming from upstairs.

In fact the poor old farmhouse, which had withstood everything nature could hoy at it for about two hundred years, with walls four feet thick, shuddered every night to the hit sounds of the era. I could never understand how anyone could write a homework essay, or solve some tricky mathematical problem with such a racket going on all around them. But apparently it was essential.

For the remainder of the time spent (often reluctantly) in the bosom of the family – that is when not actually dormant, or in a musical trance – the teenager will inevitably be BORED! Teenage boredom is a life-threatening affliction. The pathetic victim will lie sprawled on bed, sofa or floor – body limp, mouth drooped, eyes glazed – bravely, silently suffering in the company of obsolete old farts, who are totally out of touch with the real world.

"Are you alright dear . . . you don't look well . . . a touch of flu perhaps, there's a lot of it about . . . can I get you anything?"

"What? No – don't be ridiculous, it's nothing . . . you wouldn't understand!"

Too true. And it's absolutely futile to suggest any kind of activity that might just relieve this condition. It will be dismissed. Indeed, boredom will be used as a perfectly rational argument for continuing to do nowt. I seem to recall the only known cure for these bouts of rampant apathy would be the plaintive call of the telephone.

Suddenly, at the first ring-a-ding, they would move with one Olympian bound to caress and comfort the wretched thing. But then you've probably long since discovered that there's nothing quite like a deep, meaningless, whispering, sniggering two-hour phone conversation to cheer up the despondent damsel – of any age.

I was reminded of this terrible boring phenomenon recently, when I came across a league table of the most boring people. No mention of teenagers here you understand – this was concerned with professional bores, and where you might find them. According to the lady who compiled the list, first – top of the Premiership – were accountants. Alright, fair enough perhaps – I suppose their image isn't exactly dashing is it? And money can certainly be a wearisome subject, especially when you haven't got any. And those with more than enough usually talk too much about it anyway.

Second came journalists. Not sure about them, but they probably blather endlessly about all the famous folk they've interviewed, the exciting places they've been – and the fascinating in-depth piece they've just written on Gordon Brown. I imagine it could easily become a proper drag.

Third were teachers. Yes, I'll buy that. In fact maybe they should be even higher. Well, let's face it, they've got a lot going for them – long periods of inactivity, a sheltered index-linked existence, cocooned in the sanctuary of the classroom from playschool to early retirement. You'd expect them to do pretty well in such a competition.

Further down the league were stodgy politicians, humourless traffic wardens, theatrical luvvies, and pot-bellied lager louts. Surprisingly no mention of farmers at all. Perhaps the unfortunate woman hadn't met any. Well believe me, minimal research would have convinced her that whenever two or more peasants are gathered together, they are quite capable of outboring anybody, nea bother.

WE have a remarkable capacity to be truly deeply madly uninspiring. There's just so much to be tedius about. The weather (naturally), sheep of course, the harvest, yesterday's weather, the Common Market, lambing, the price of mule gimmers at Scot's Gap, the long-term weather forecast . . . Oh yes, we can go on and on, till the cows LEAVE home!

But wait a minute, hang on – the list is incomplete; there's another group who can probably beat the lot. Maybe you've guessed already. Right – it's those desperate multicoloured masochists, who every weekend 'tame' 18 holes with a net 95, and then insist on reliving every hook, slice and socket again and again. Find yourself a twittering golfing peasant, and I suspect you've got a potential champion.

Which reminds me, did I ever tell you about the fantastic five iron I hit at the twelfth last week? No? Well, you'll not believe it, but I'll tell y'anyway. Howlin' gale, pourin' wi' rain – the ball stuck in a divot – a hundred and fifty yards to go and . . .

Whoops – see what I mean?

Joseph's Tale

SO the first question I ask myself is, how did Joseph Brewis get from Wooler to Liverpool in the spring of 1855?

I'm just guessing you understand, but chances are this country boy had never been any further than Berwick and Alnwick before this adventure. And yet, I suspect he might have been thinking about flitting the nest for some time.

Well, look at it this way. There he was pushing 30, unmarried, still living with mother and the rest of the brood. The auld man, poor fella, dead this last 10 years – only 39 when the influenza, or consumption, or some mad bullock got 'im – leaving Jane with five kids, to make the best of it on a few acres at East Lilburn.

By now Joe's two older brothers both had wives and families, and the two younger sisters were still at home as well. Too many mouths to feed. The farm couldn't support all of them, and being the youngest son, he seemed to get all the mucky jobs, and the leftovers at suppertime. No, there wasn't much future for him here. Arguably, he'd stayed long enough already.

Of course, then again, I might have got it all wrong. It could be much simpler than that. It's just possible Joseph was nothing more than a right randy little peasant. There might've been a whole gaggle of distressed milkmaids, all with a bun in the oven, waddling about the byways round Chatton and Wooperton. Perhaps a posse of irate fathers was even now loading shotguns, sharpening pitchforks. Maybe he was obliged to leave in haste – how do I know?

Anyway, whatever the reason, it would surely be a gigantic leap for Joseph. With a wee bundle of clothes, a handful of sovereigns, and very little idea of what lies over the hill, he sets off in late March, leaving his brothers to cope with the lambing.

He walks, or gets a lift on a cart, as far as the Tankerville in Wooler, and there catches the coach to Newcastle. I imagine it might take most of the day . . . It's a lump of 50 miles, with maybe a stop in Morpeth for a pie and a pint at the Queen's. It's not till the team trots into the Haymarket at dusk, and he gets his first whiff of the noisy smelly city, that he begins to wonder if he made the right decision.

However, let's assume he's a big strong lad, he can look after himself, and before dusk he finds lodgings for the night at The Farmer's Rest. It seems an appropriate hostelry for such a traveller. He hardly sleeps, though. There's too much going on outside, and inside his head. He knows tomorrow will be special. He's about to risk life and limb on the railway.

The Newcastle to Carlisle line had opened 15 years earlier. Of course our hero had never seen the great smoking beast up Wooler way, but he'd heard all about this sophisticated modern mode of transport. Faster, smoother, cheaper than a horse, they said, and it would get him over to the west coast. Then all he had to do was find another night's lodging in Carlisle, and shuffle down the Great Western track to Liverpool.

Whatever happened, he had to be at the docks on April 4. That was absolutely essential. A day late, and the whole dream was shattered. Joseph made it alright, but I wonder what his thoughts were as he walked up the gangplank. Would he ever survive the journey? It was unlikely that everybody would. His last chance to turn back . . .

The good ship Marco Polo – 1,625 tons, Captain James Clarke – sailed out of the Mersey on April 5, 1855, bound for Australia. The passenger list records nine privileged travellers in cabins and a total of 410 other passengers, presumably packed somewhere, anywhere below deck. These included "Joseph Brewis, aged 29 years, English, occupation gentleman, parents Joseph senior and Jane (nee Maddison). Full fare of twenty pounds paid before departure".

Perhaps Joe found a pal among his fellow migrants, another brave or desperate soul setting off for a new life on the other side of the world. In such crowded, sweaty, cheek-by-jowl conditions, they'd certainly have to have a sense of humour. Even so, I expect there'd be a few punch-ups, and maybe the odd romance, before the ship reached its destination. They were all destined to be in that same boat for about a hundred days. It could take four months.

No QANTAS jumbo with a leggy stewardess serving Fosters. No luxury liner with cocktails every time the sun crossed the yardarm. No Suez Canal yet – that short cut didn't open until 1869. So the Marco Polo would turn, tack, and toss her way through the angry Bay of Biscay, down the Atlantic coast of Africa, round the Cape of Good Hope, across the vast Indian Ocean, over the Great Australian Bight. She would battle through breeze and wind and gale, eventually dropping anchor at Melbourne in late June.

The story goes that somehow Joseph jumped ship before that, at a place 200 miles to the west called Portland, and walked the 50 miles inland to Hamilton. His plan was to get a job on the Mokanga cattle station at Karabeal, run by a family called Churnside. Maybe he had an introduction, perhaps there'd been some earlier correspondence, or he might simply have heard about the job on the ship.

Whatever – he missed the Mokanga bullock team by a few hours, and set off on foot to follow their tracks into the hinterland. Legend has it he spent at least one night up a gum tree, scared half t'death at his first sighting of an aborigine. He was a long way from Wooler!

Nevertheless, he caught up with the lads a few days later, went to work, and eventually married a lass called Mary Lord in 1860. Her father owned the only pub in nearby Cavendish. No fool, Joseph. Indeed, the courting of Mr Lord's daughter was a shrewd move altogether. As well as the hotel, the Lords owned grazing land in the area, and Joseph and Mary subsequently settled on a section of land at Cranridge. Within five years of leaving Northumberland he was a farmer again.

They produced seven children. The eldest, Sarah Jane, was followed by six brothers; the youngest, Samuel, was born in 1871. Their descendants still live in Victoria, most of them sheep farmers (will they never learn?). One of them wrote to me recently with the bare bones of this story. He knew his great-grandfather had emigrated in 1855, but whereabouts in England had he come from? They had no idea. They might never have known, had not Mary Brewis from Melbourne paused for one night last year on her journey into Scotland, at a farmhouse b-and-b near Hexham. She subsequently reported back home that Northumbria was awash with

Brewises – most of 'em farmers, and one of them had Joseph on his family tree.

The thing that hits me about this tale is the guts, the balls of such folk as Joseph. Nowadays it's so quick and easy to fly around the world, and (if you can afford it) in first class luxury. Teenage kids stuff a clean T-shirt into a bag, and just go. All of us can zoom to London in three hours, hop on a flight to Australia, and be there (albeit jet-lagged) the next day.

But when Joe made the trip 140 years ago, it was barely the same world. Queen Victoria ruled half of it, and her army was fighting in the Crimea. This was before the Indian Mutiny or the American Civil War. Gold had only just been discovered in California (and Australia). Only 20 years earlier the Tolpuddle Martyrs had been deported in chains.

A whole century before Joseph Brewis set sail, my own peasant ancestor, Thomas, was farming at North Whitehouse, Stannington, and paying rent to the Earl of Carlisle. At the same time, just over the field at Dovecote farm, his brother Robert was a tenant of the same landlord. This fellow Robert was Joseph's great-grandfather.

Alright, so Joseph's branch of the family floated all the way to the antipodes. And mine? Well, it seems to have taken nearly 300 years to struggle 10 miles up the road, and we're still here.

Beetle-Mania

I TELL myself it's perfectly natural to be wary, cautious, even a little fearful of things y'knaa nowt aboot.

Well, let's face it – if you're not just a wee bit inhibited by ignorance, then you should've been a politician (or else you're very young). And as I get older I realise how little I know. Knowledge expands as we shrink (Henry's last theorem).

Especially, it's this burgeoning high-tech communications revolution that fills me with awe and apprehension. But for someone trained as a 'dog 'n' stick man', perhaps this is not altogether surprising. If the world is now zooming along on the information highway, alas, I'm still stuck behind a tractor on a narrow back road somewhere between (say) Warkworth and Guyzance.

Indeed, I can remember when having a telephone in the house meant you were no end of a swell. Later (about the time of the Coronation, I suppose) the definitive sign of sophistication was probably a telly – the bigger and the uglier the better. After that, draw up your own list – videos, computer, fax, whatever.

But once upon a time washing day was always on a Monday, and my granny's phone number was Shilbottle double two. We were Shilbottle two-six. Today that old homestead boasts eleven figures. Eleven! Life has more numbers by the minute. Digital diarrhoea!

Nowadays, when I'm obliged to dial some city office, a disembodied female Dalek invariably asks me to "hold", plays me The Dance of the Sugar Plum Fairy, invites me to press the star on my machine, asks awkward questions, demands immediate answers – if yes, press three, or five, or speak now – then tells me I'm in a queue! I'm not in a bloody queue! I've rarely been seen in a queue. I hate queues. I'm in the kitchen with a fag and a cuppa tea to steady m'nerves before I made the call in the first place!

I phoned son and heir recently. "This will be costing you a fortune," he said after about ten minutes' blather. "Why don't you use e-mail?" His concern was touching, and as he lives in the middle of Africa (twelve digits – only one more than Shilbottle) I decided to investigate this phenomenon.

A neighbouring tycoon had all the gear. "Tell me your message," he says, "and it will be with the lad within minutes – price of a local call."

So I'm standing there, all open-mouthed bewilderment, while he types the deathless prose on to his processor, brings it up on the screen for my

127

approval, then presses another appropriate button. The amazing contraption makes a few weird noises (rather like my tummy after garlic prawns and half a carafe of house red), declares my communiqué is safely despatched into the system, and that's it – nothing more to be done. Magic.

In no time at all my message is on an African screen, and son can respond as he sees fit. How does it work? Don't ask. I'm writing this with a ball-point pen: that's clever enough for me. Perhaps the first time I came upon this ever-growing technological monster was way back, when I was a proper peasant. For some reason I found myself on a regional advisory committee to a large agricultural co-operative. Heaven knows why I was elected. Maybe I wasn't. Maybe no-one else in his right mind wanted to be on the committee.

Anyway, we noble band of chattering farmers met once a quarter to discuss current trends in the business, and how this far-sighted company might best keep in touch with the grass roots, and service their valued customers. The company seldom listened to anything we said, of course, and I realise now it was little more than a P.R. exercise for them, and an ego trip for us. Nevertheless we were made to feel very important, and better still given a slap-up lunch at a fancy hotel.

On one of these high-falutin' occasions we were at The George at Chollerford, and as we came out into the car park I was chatting to the chairman, and happened to mention (as one does) that I was extremely worried about m'turnips.

It was a warm growthy spring, and a plague of ravenous flea beetles had swept up from County Durham intent on devouring every wee bagie plant north of the Tyne. It appeared only one thing could stop them, and this was a lethal anti-flea beetle spray called (I think) Didimac. Sounds an unlikely name, I admit, but it was something silly like that.

"I expect we'll have it in stock," smiled the chairman confidently. "Our pesticide expert will certainly be aware of the problem, and may well have cornered the market in Didimac. I doubt if anyone else has any."

A few other farmers had gathered by now, and were expressing their concern too. Reports of the beetle scourge were spreading rapidly. In fact, if you were a young emerging turnip it was very bad news. Your life expectancy was measured in hours. A shower of Didimac was the only salvation.

"No need to worry," said the chairman. "We've recently installed a new super computerised data system – state of the art – way ahead of its time." He was preening himself. "You may not believe this," he said smugly, "but we can now dial a special number from anywhere in the U.K., feed in the selected code, and within seconds have detailed information on any product you care to mention. Availability, cost, delivery – everything.

"I can do it now. It could save you boys a whole lot of hassle. You can go straight to whichever branch or depot has the stuff in stock and collect it. Simple."

With that he strode purposefully back into the hotel and picked up the phone in the foyer – it was before the days when everybody had a mobile phone. We followed. He dialled the special number, and waited. After a lot of spluttering and a rising concerto of expletives, it became clear our man was having some bother. Seemed the new super computerised system worked fine, but there was no Didimac in any of the firm's umpteen branches.

"There's been unprecendented demand further south," he stammered. "It's all gone. We're ordering fresh supplies, of course, but it could take a day or two . . ." The poor fellow was obviously well embarrassed. A vast organisation like this, enormous investment in fancy new equipment – but they couldn't produce a sniff of Didimac at a time when everybody was crying out for it. Disgraceful. Could be a disaster, like the locusts in Egypt!

On the way home, muttering miserably to m'self – pictures in my head of fifteen acres of healthy, green, neatly rowed-up plants being consumed by beetles, convinced I was on the brink of financial ruin (again) – I called in at the local store in Scot's Gap.

In those days this was little more than a black wooden hut crammed full of string and wire and wellies, and a few other agricultural necessities. (The black hut is still there, but the business has blossomed somewhat since then).

"Didimac?" I asked without much optimism.

"Aye, been a big rush on the stuff," said Andy. "Sold the last can half an hour ago. Everybody wants it. Those flea beetles must be goin' mad this year."

Panic. If I'd stayed at home instead of gettin' all tarted up and trailing off to that poncey committee meeting I could have had the last can. I swear I could hear the damned insects munching away on my snadgers just down the road. The wee winged beasties would all have evil grins on their faces, and be as fat and full as flea beetles could be. It was a catastrophe.

"Steady on," says Andy. "I think I know where there'll be some. There's this great big warehouse in Middlesbrough . . ."

"Middlesbrough!" I squealed. It might as well be in Ethiopia. It could take weeks to get it. Certainly I wouldn't dare drive into Middlesbrough m'self. Middlesbrough was on the other side of hell. Images of vast industrial desert, belching chemical factories, millions of strange people, a maze of sinister streets. No grass. The great ICI empire was somewhere down there, wasn't it? Nobody I knew had ever been to Middlesbrough – let alone come out again carrying a can of Didimac! The beetles had won.

The Scot's Gap man looked at me with a sympathy he reserved for really desperate gibbering clients. "We'll get it for you – how much do you need?" he said quietly, picking up the phone. "Should be with you first thing tomorrow. You'll have the turnips sprayed by dinnertime. No problem."

I wasn't convinced. How could this little rural family outfit – operating from a shack in the middle of nowhere, with hardly any computerised bleeping things – succeed where the great Agric Co-op, awash with all its twentieth century wizardry, had failed?

In fact, what happened went something like this. Scot's Gap man called his cousin Gloria (that might not have been her name, but who cares?). Gloria worked somewhere near the warehouse, and simply walked down the road and got a can of beetle killer. She put it on the Number 27 bus to the Haymarket in Newcastle and phoned her brother Willie. Willie picked it up from the depot as he came off his late shift, and made sure it got on to a mate's wagon heading for Morpeth.

Early next morning somebody took it down to the post office in Oldgate, where Jakie the postman was about to set off on his wanderings up the Wansbeck valley. I discovered the package by the sheep pens at the farm gate about 8am. There was no extra delivery charge.

End of story. End of flea beetles. Total happiness.

The moral of this tale (if there is one) is yours to unravel. But it might have something to do with clever gadgets and canny folk.

130

Call Of The Wild

I WAS intrigued by a recent report from an agricultural correspondent somewhere in Somerset or Gloucestershire (I think). Certainly it was one of those far-off counties in the deep cotton-pickin' south, way beyond Darlington.

It appears a farmer in those parts bought a herd of dairy cows from Normandy. He shipped them across the channel, and after a lorry ride up the motorway, the French ladies eventually stepped out on to a patch of England's green and pleasant pasture. Almost immediately they began to graze, chew the cud, and contemplate their new home, apparently none the worse for the journey. So far so good.

The problems began on that first evening when the farmer went to call them in for milking. He opened the gate and shouted the usual encouraging noises, promising delicious high protein dairy nuts and a little gentle mammary relief. But he got no response. No matter how hard he tried to cajole them, no matter how persuasive or desperate he sounded, these cows didn't move. They simply stared at the poor bloke with blank expressions, and maybe the occasional bewildered Gallic shrug.

Finally, as the sun began to set somewhere over Wales, our man was obliged to summon his dog, the missus, two teenage kids, a neighbour, and a whole lot of Anglo-Saxon expletives, in order to round up his new herd and drive them out of the field and into the byre. Worse was to follow.

Once into the milking parlour the animals behaved well enough. They duly lined up in the stalls, ate the tempting grub set before them, and allowed themselves to be attached to the milking machines. However, they all stubbornly declined to give any milk. Well, I suppose they must have given some, but apparently it took ages to squeeze much more than a cupfull from each. Disaster! Complete lack of entente cordiale! This seriously unproductive exercise continued for several days. The cows were obviously bursting with milk, and the farmer almost exploding with frustration. What to do? Faced with the prospect of a quick cardiac and/or economic ruin, he desperately sought professional advice.

Exactly where he found it I know not but, as you will be aware, there are now 'counsellors' available for every problem under the sun, and perhaps a Bovine Therapy Unit lurks somewhere in the Min. of Ag. Anyway, the answer was simple and straightforward. These were French cows, were they not? Well then, you have to speak their language. It is totally unreasonable to expect bilingual bovines. In such circumstances one is obliged to parlais francais, monsieur . . .

So next morning our farmer friend went out into the field armed with a French phrase book and, somewhat self-consciously, tried a new Euro approach.

"Alors, mes petites vaches," he called. "Venez avec moi, s'il vous plaît." He was trying as hard as he could to sound like Maurice Chevalier and, sure enough, first reactions were quite encouraging, so he pressed on.

"Allez, allez," he shouted. "La plume de ma tante . . . vive de Gaulle."

And what do you know? Les vaches pricked up their floppy French lugs and proceeded to trot happily into the byre. What's more, suitably relaxed, they readily produced great churnfuls of milk. Problem solved. End of story. Fade out to strains of Edith Piaf singing: "Je ne regrette rien" – or even a quick burst of La Marseillaise!

This true story immediately reminded me of two weird little agricultural words which I had assumed stockmen everywhere always used to call their cattle. Perhaps the fellow in Somerset wasn't a proper peasant – but I'm pretty confident that if you asked any of your farming friends what their cattle call is they would, without hesitation, utter a rather strange noise which sounds like "Huff-oaff . . . Huff-oaff".

Yes, I know. You may well ask. I haven't a clue what it means, where it came from, or even if I've spelt it properly. But that's it. That's the call for cattle. Believe me: always has been since – well, forever, I think – certainly hereabouts.

For umpteen generations peasant offspring have first learned to say "Mummy" and "Daddy" (just like every other normal smelly child) and

132

then "Huff-oaff". This as they followed grandad to feed the calves, or move some bullocks from one field to another.

I had just understood, without really thinking about it, that farmers (and cows) the world over would know the "Huff-oaff" sound. But maybe not. Obviously it means nothing to a French cow, which is only further confirmation (if it were needed) that we should have nowt more to do with the European Union.

However, before any bunny-huggin' cow-cuddlin' townie reader dashes out into the fields and byways, gaily calling "Huff-oaff" to every bunch of grazing cattle they see, a word of warning. The response may not always be predictable. You see, it largely depends on the type of animal – and especially how hungry it is.

Well-fed dairy cows are pretty docile as a rule. They usually have a rather smug self-satisfied look about them, confident in the knowledge they'll be milked and fed twice a day, every day of the year. On the other hand, other breeds – particularly the suckler cow variety (the sort who rear a massive beef calf oot-bye in the wind and rain) – are generally in such a state of ravenous anxiety, they might well gallop all over you if there's the remotest chance of finding a mouldy Malteser in your anorak pocket.

On a bleak winter's day when there's little or no grass to chew, the suckler and her mates will be poised at the gateway, bellies deep in slurry, waiting for the next relief delivery of hay or silage. It wouldn't matter if you called in Swahili or Serbo-Croat, or sang a refrain from Madam Butterfly – even the far-off sound of a spluttering tractor is enough to conjure visions of more food, and inspire a frantic stampede. Indeed, the experienced stockman knows he has but the blink of an eye to unload the trailer and flee, or they'll have the coat off his back.

While we're on the subject – as you might imagine, the call for a flock of sheep is quite different. The words are from the same silly farming lexicon, of course, and equally meaningless. Our devoted shepherd will also have been taught, from an age when he barely reached the top of Dad's wellies, that to summon the yowes frea the knowes he should shout "Kep, kep, kep".

What sort of gripping intellectual dialogue ensued would probably depend on the enthusiasm of the sheep's response, the behaviour of the collie dog, the weather, and perhaps how many nasty final demands the postman delivered that morning. Nevertheless, take my word for it, if you need to attract the attention of the average mule yow, you should at least begin negotiations with "Kep, kep, kep". Honest!

It's a while since I had much to do with horses, and the memories are mostly painful. In my experience the horse may not be the brightest of God's creatures, but without doubt all have achieved an A-level in awkwardness. What's more, they are far too big and strong and ugly to mess about with. That's if you can ever catch the brute in the first place.

"Cup, cup, cup . . .", or perhaps a sort of clicking noise with your tongue, I remember as the idiotic gee-gee call, and although Prince (or whoever) may well react at the speed of light, it is only to steal the goodies you have in the bucket. Try to put a halter round his neck or a saddle on his back, and he's just as likely to knock you down, devour the tempting morsels, playfully kick you in the goolies and retire to the far end of the croft, sniggering.

And yet (strangely) the countryside is awash with galloping equine evangelists who believe the horse to be the result of some divine handiwork. One must beware the blinkered enthusiasm of battle-scarred colonels and their winsome womenfolk sitting 17 hands above reality, convinced (poor things) the world is made up entirely of fetlocks and withers and three-day events.

Disregard anything demure young Abigail, kitted out in designer jodhpurs and hard hat, tells you about her lovable Thelwellian friend. Sooner or later that spherical four-legged sod will hoy her off and trample her into the clarts once too often. This is usually the moment when many nubile horsey gals eventually see the light and transfer their deeper affections to a nearby spotty youth, leaving mother to muck out the stable, and daddy inclined to barbecue the beast. I've been there.

So be warned. Your rural vocabulary may have been expanded a little today, but there are real dangers associated with these peculiar new words. It might be when next roamin' in the country you are inclined to utter a few furtive "Huff-oaffs" or "Kep, keps" – and find yourself suddenly surrounded by assorted curious cuddly livestock. On the other hand, you could be overwhelmed and relieved of your last Rolo.

It's a jungle out there, I tell you!

Moving Pictures

SAMUEL was first off the minibus as it pulled up by the church. A dozen members of the Percy Street painting class followed him out on to the grass verge.

They stretched stiff limbs, rubbed tummies, blew noses, and generally rearranged themselves after the journey . . . chattering, looking about at the village. A couple of old blokes hurriedly lit up (no smoking allowed on the bus, of course) and one or two mature ladies were already enquiring about toilet facilities.

Paint boxes, brushes, easels, little folding stools, and other sundry bits of artists' paraphernalia were unloaded and sorted, ready to begin this week's 'masterpiece'. Mr Wilkinson, the tutor, was waving his arms about and making suggestions.

"A scene by the river perhaps, with the bridge in the foreground? (But remember water can be a difficult subject, especially when it's moving.) The 13th century church maybe – from somewhere among those old tombstones? Or why not just a nice Northumbrian landscape looking west – hedges, walls, patchwork fields, high clouds – that sort of thing?"

Sam knew exactly what he was going to do. Nowt! He had a sketch pad in his coat pocket, but he wasn't really in a drawing mood today. To be honest he was never much cop as an artist anyway. He knew that.

Not like Mrs Tanner and Walter Armstrong. Real arty-farty pair, those two. Even been known to sell the occasional watercolour in Whitley Bay. He definitely wasn't in that league. But as he said: "It was always somethin' to do of a Tuesday. Meet different folk, get away from the damn city once in a while."

And he was certainly determined to be on this trip. Well, this was his midden, wasn't it? He was born just up the road, went to school here, worked at the Vicarage Farm most of his life. And a canny country life it was too, until he lost his missus a few years back and was persuaded "t'move in wi' the dowta".

He hadn't liked that flittin' much, and suspected Sandra and her man weren't all that thrilled about it either. But what else could he do? Too old for farm work, the boss needed the house, and there was nowhere to rent around here. Not in this village, not these days. It was Sandra's spare room or Happy Valley Retirement Home – and he wasn't ready for that, not yet.

So, hands in pockets, cap on the back of his head, his mind full of rusty jumbled-up memories, Samuel set off by himself up the road towards the old school house. He'd never had the heart to come back here until today.

There'd be a few changes likely. He knew the post office had gone, the redundant reverend removed from his vicarage and replaced by an accountant, the local copper promoted to Panda patrol. And of course he knew St Aidan's Primary had long since closed its doors to the handful of little snotty-nosed country kids, and become some newcomer's des. res.

It still looked remarkably like a village school though, at least to Samuel's eye it did. The high windows that ensured yesterday's children weren't distracted by the outside world were still in place. Leaning on the wall, he was surprised to hear himself reciting "seven eights are fifty-six, eight eights are sixty-four" – sing-songing it out loud – and looked anxiously around in case he'd been overheard. But only a black labrador barked at him from the garden, and that didn't count. In fact, apart from some of the art group wandering about, the village seemed pretty well deserted.

He stared wistfully for a few minutes at the old building, and wondered if the giggling ghosts of Miss Thompson's class still lingered there. He noted the boys' bog had been demolished (understandably). The small concrete yard had become a patio with

136

potted plants, and there was a thatched bird table under the conker tree, where he once kissed a nine-year-old nymphet called Peggy Prentice.

Just over the road, where the lads used to play football with coats as goalposts and the lasses skipped to half-forgotten rhymes, three new houses were almost completed. They were big brash mini-mansions with important-looking front doors. Each stood in about a quarter of an acre, with double garage and conservatory, stone-built to satisfy the planners and blend into the environment. Maybe they would some day, Sam reckoned – in about a hundred years or so.

He sauntered up to the corner where Beech Cottage stood. He'd always had a fancy to end his days in this place. It was the garden as much as anything that appealed to him. Bobby Whelan generally had the earliest taties, the champion leeks, the sweetest onions.

But such dreams were obviously well out of date now. The builders had transformed the modest abode into something only a tycoon could afford. Quite unrecognisable. A posh red gravelled driveway, and a complete new wing spread all over Bobby's magic vegetable patch, almost to the roadside.

It had been advertised as: "A superior rural residence in much sought-after Northumbrian village, sympathetically restored, with delightful views over rolling countryside." Samuel had seen the agent's extravagant prose in the local paper, and couldn't believe it was the same Beech Cottage he knew. But it was.

Huh – just wait till Murphy's coal wagon went straight on at the bend some frosty February morning, and ended up in their sympathetically decorated luxury lounge. He allowed himself a wicked little snigger at the prospect and moved on, muttering quietly.

Beech Cottage, Glebe Cottage, Dene Cottage, Quarry Cottage – the parish had always been littered with quaint wee dwellings, built to house a regiment of weather-beaten worthies who once served the estate as gamekeeper, groom, forester or farmworker.

There was a time, Samuel recalled, when bonnie young lasses and bold country callants could always find work up at the hall. An era when a staff of 30 or more scuttled about curtsying, tugging forelocks and generally ensuring the Broome-Handleburys lived the life of privileged gentlefolk. Not so long ago either.

Sam remembered both his parents spending most of their lives at "The Big Hoose" – father as one of half a dozen gardeners, mother with her sleeves rolled up in that vast white-tiled kitchen, gutting fish, pheasant, grouse, venison, rabbit and hare (long before the myxi came, of course). She brought some of the grub home occasionally.

No, it wasn't such a bad life, in spite of what some people said. A steady job, a few tasty scraps from the rich man's table, a rent-free roof over your head. The system worked well enough then. In fact, you could argue the Broome-Handleburys (and their like, with all their old money) kept the countryside ticking and turning for several generations.

Funny how things can change, though. Now their stately home was open to the public at weekends to pay for a new roof, and that kitchen was a curiosity - a museum. Aye, it was new money in the parish now, Sam could see that. Feudal yesterday, fashionable today. City folk were moving in, and who could blame them? He would've lived here for ever if he could.

The new home at 57 Gladstone Terrace (even with central heating and a bookie within spittin' distance) held few attractions for him. There was no garden for a start. You stepped straight out the front door on to the street. Above all he missed his own air space.

He'd always needed trees and grass (hadn't realised it before – took it all for granted). He needed quiet neighbours, not too close. Somewhere to wander and talk to himself. The odd secret hidey-hole where he could sit and watch Mother Nature change her clothes, see swallows come and go, hear a cuckoo and a curlew. Ye gods, was he turning into some sort of romantic, he wondered? A bit late in the day, wasn't it?

Out of the village Samuel turned down Purdy's Lonnen. He liked this little lane. It led to nowhere really, wasn't on any maps, the council surveyor probably didn't know it existed – just a narrow overgrown track 'twixt two more important roads heading for more important places.

Here the verges were uncut, unsprayed – full of fescues, Yorkshire fog, dockens, cow parsley, aromatic meadowsweet, six-foot-high hemlock, and a host of other plants he'd been familiar with since childhood but couldn't put a name to.

You seldom met a soul down here – that was another great attraction. On a real bad day there might be a courtin' couple snoggin' in a steamed-up car, a bramble picker who'd discovered 'El Dorado', or a wayward rep

138

desperately phoning head office on his mobile, lost. Put them all together and the lane almost took on the menace of the motorway. But that was a rare event.

The brothers Purdy had farmed the Grange at the bottom end of the lonnen, way back some time between the wars. Legend had it that the two men seldom got on, argued and fought endlessly. Didn't like work very much. Spent their days racing ponies up and down the lane, and boozing in the Wheatheads every night.

They never married, and lived in rustic squalor surrounded by dirty dishes, broken scraps of furniture and smelly collie dogs. Seems they did once inherit a Victorian bedroom suite from a deceased relative and, having dragged the various pieces upstairs, discovered the massive mahogany wardrobe wouldn't quite fit under the beamed ceiling. Somewhat disenchanted by this unforeseen problem, each man grabbed an axe, and together they angrily hacked away at the beams until the disobliging wardrobe could eventually be stood up against the wall.

As far as Sam was aware, that bedroom at the Grange still bore the scars of the Purdy's D-I-Y, and the quiet lonnen still bore their name. Now that was really serious fame, wasn't it? Fancy having a country lane named after you, eh? Better by far than some crummy housing estate or a street. That was nowt special. Who was Gladstone anyway?

Then he saw the fox. He probably wouldn't have noticed him at all if it hadn't been for the four squawking crows harassing the old dog, but there they were at the edge of the wood, giving the beast a whole lot of grief. Swooping down on him, even strutting arrogantly around, right up to his nose end.

Were the birds intent on doing Foxy some serious mischief? Sam wondered. Surely the poor fellow must be injured, half shot, or poisoned perhaps. Why didn't he just run off?

Samuel was pondering on this when the mystery was just as suddenly solved. With a final irritated snarl and a flourish of his bushy tail, the fox quickly darted off into the trees, carrying the remains of an unlucky rabbit in his jaws! Ah, so that's what it was all about – he should've known. The corbies were simply after a free lunch.

Samuel unwrapped the bait Sandra had prepared for him, and chewed on an apple as he strode along the bottom road towards Vicarage Farm. Not that he considered it a "proper" farm any more – just a muckle new concrete shed and wall-to-wall cereals as far as he could see. Not as it was in the good old days, when he worked there among the cows and yowes and sows. And look at all those old stone hemmels, 'tastefully' converted into smart commuter homes now.

An elegant lady wearing green gloves was gardening behind what had once been the cow byre. "You might not believe it," Sam shouted towards her, "but I've mucked out your sittin' room many's the time!"

She looked up, smiling like a TV presenter, and said: "What? Yes, isn't it a lovely day" and concentrated on her bedding plants again, wondering briefly who the stranger might be. One of those nosy ramblers, probably.

Sam quickened his pace and headed for the Wheatheads. Geordie would be there for sure. Together they'd put the world t' rights, have a smoke and down a couple of pints. It would be good to see his old mate again. He ordered the ale from a landlord he didn't recognise and, leaning on the bar, looked around the room. In fact he didn't recognise anybody – and Geordie wasn't there.

"George Wilkinson?" said the barman, opening a bottle of Chardonnay for a very smart retired couple sitting by the window. "Haven't seen him for ages. I think they got a council flat in Cramlington".

140

Samuel suddenly didn't fancy a second pint. He went to the gents instead, and then wandered rather forlornly back towards the church. The artists were already gathering to go home, comparing their day's work – talking intensely about light, and shade, and perspective.

"A thoroughly charming little village, you'll agree," Mr Wilkinson spread his arms expansively. "So full of character and history and rural tranquillity, isn't it?" he twittered – just as two Tornado jets screamed past his left lug, and rendered him temporarily speechless.

"Magnificent old church," declared Walter Armstrong, "though I fear I've barely done it justice today . . ." No-one thought he was serious.

Samuel climbed aboard the bus and sat on his blank sketch pad, staring at his boots. "Did you get a good picture then?" asked Mrs Tanner brightly, as she shuffled her large bottom next to his.

Sam gave her a melancholy look. "Aye, well now, come t' think of it pet," he said quietly, "I think maybe I did . . ."

★　★　★